What's the Matter With Batman?

ROBIN S. ROSENBERG

What's the Matter With Batman?

An Unauthorized Clinical Look Under the Mask of the Caped Crusader

Robin S. Rosenberg, Ph.D.

Foreword by Dennis O'Neil

ROBIN S. ROSENBERG

ISBN: 1477478558
ISBN-13: 978-1477478554

Dedication

To Stephen, with love

ROBIN S. ROSENBERG

TABLE OF CONTENTS

ROBIN S. ROSENBERG

FOREWORD

By Dennis O'Neil

If anyone knows Batman well (aside for Alfred), it's Dennis O'Neil. As writer and editor of Batman comic book stories and novels, he is responsible for some of the psychological depth in Batman's stories—Batman's gritty but realistic emotions and his psychological conflicts. And he understands why we are interested in Batman.

If our psychologist brothers and sisters are correct, and surely they are, your first encounter with stories didn't involve words because you didn't know any. You were new to the world, an enormous source of pride to your parents, no doubt, and you were doing your job. Which was to learn. You lay there amid sheet and blanket being adorable and looked and tried to make some sense of what you saw, and eventually you did, at least a little.

--If I make noise, the big person will pick me up and put something nice in my mouth and go kitchy koo...

So you might have said if you'd had words, which you didn't, as you began to know what to do and, incidentally, to construct a very rough first draft of your autobiography—your very own story. Pretty soon, patterns began to emerge, you got a sense of cause-and-effect and then you were crawling and tap dancing and running for office and evolving into the splendid piece of the universe you are now.

But you weren't done with stories when Daddy stowed your buggy in the attic. You created your personal narratives and from these you cobbled together your identity: whom others think you are, who *you* think you are. Barring major life-upset, this jury-rigged self does the job just fine. It gives you somebody to be and you continue to embellish and edit that self's story without even realizing you're telling a tale.

Storytelling goes back a long way, both in your life and in the saga of the human race. Like almost everything that has lasted and lasted and lasted, it helped our hunting and gathering forebears survive.

Recognizing patterns and understanding cause-and-effect helped them avoid becoming entrees and sharing stories, maybe around campfires, helped elders unite the tribe, and giving names to thunder and flood and wind and the thousands of inexplicable misfortunes that beset the tribe, and from the names conjuring personalities for them, gave everyone at least the illusion of control. *If you can name it, maybe it'll listen to your pleas…*

The earth churned and men struggled and prevailed and people's stories transformed into hundreds of different forms and we eventually learned to write our stories and then duplicate the writing and finally, late in 1938 or early in 1939, two young guys who lived in New York City and were trying to establish themselves in the publishing business created a character who was called, after a false start or two, the Bat-Man. This Bat-Man of theirs first appeared in what was in those pre-war-years, a new medium: comic books—an amalgam of language and image put to the old, old use of telling stories. Comic books had predecessors, of course, including the comic *strips* that appeared in virtually every major urban newspaper. But comic *books*, containing several original self-contained stories that spanned genres and were intended for newsstand sale—these were a new game in town, one that Bill Finger and Bob Kane played pretty well from the beginning.

"The Bat-Man," with script by Finger and art by Kane, made his debut in *Detective Comics #27*, in a six-page story called "The Case of the Chemical Syndicate" that owed some debt to a popular radio and magazine character, The Shadow. The Bat-Man was yet another iteration of a popular kind of hero, the playboy crime-solver—rich, idle, adventurous, happy to help the somewhat dim policemen catch miscreants. Like many similar characters—the Shadow, Zorro, the Scarlet Pimpernel, et al—this Bat-Man of Finger and Kane had a double identity and hid behind a disguise when he was discomfiting bad guys. What made him absolutely perfect for the new comic books was that disguise: not just a mask, but a costume that was striking and unique and so was ideal for a medium in which at least half of the storytelling was done in pictures. He was an instant icon and for comics...what could be better?

But, great duds notwithstanding, he was still a rich kid whose hobby happened to be vigilantism.

Until the fifth story in a long, long, continuing series. Bill Finger gave his readers what would soon be a staple of superheroics (and has been important in most of the world's mythologies): the origin story. Young Bruce Wayne, a child, sees his parents killed during a mugging and thereafter devotes himself to symbolically avenging that atrocity and, perhaps not incidentally, doing what he can to prevent other children from suffering as he has suffered. Like the costume: perfect.

The Bat-Man became Batman and prospered, appearing in, by now, thousands of comics, and on radio and television and in novels and short stories and...what are we forgetting?—oh yeah: movies. Big, big movies. Along that 73-plus year journey, he's changed as he's been interpreted by different creators working for diverse audiences. He has recapitulated your own journey, from mute baby who wasn't even aware that it was trying to *understand*, to make sense of the jumble *out there*. And both of you, Batman and yourself, have recapitulated our species's involvement with stories, which began with naming mysteries and millennia later provided us with the works of Shakespeare, *War and Peace* and *Jackass: The Movie*, among many other diversions.

All three—Batman, the human race and you—have this in common: you've become increasingly complex.

Let's concentrate, finally, on Batman who is, after all, the subject of this excellent book. He has had more than a handful of personalities: playboy sleuth, cop, civic booster, alien fighter, time traveler, comedian, ratiocinator, lab technician, martial artist, father figure…(Do you see something of yourself here? Didn't you go through phases that you outgrew and would rather forget?) But for the past 40 years, give or take, there has been a general consensus. Not everyone has agreed with this general consensus, and movies exist to prove that, and the consensus is pretty loose; a lot of details aren't consistent.

But, allowing for the odd anomaly or two, here is a Batman who evolved from Bill Finger's early scripts to a layered and complicated creation, partly through a process that mimics the way ancient myths passed from bard to bard each of whom added and subtracted and redacted according to individual preferences until someone got around to writing the material down. A lot of people have written, or otherwise contributed to, the Batman mythos, taking from their predecessors what they liked, what made for good drama, what fit into their own vision of what and who this character should be. And at the end of this long process, at the end of decades…behold! A Batman! One we can work with, one we can live with, one that will serve all the masters— publishers, editors, filmmakers, toy manufacturers, and on and on—to which modern multimedia heroes are beholden. One we can agree on. And one that is still changing and won't be the same this time next year.

But for now: we have a Batman who reflects great chunks of our world and a Batman who has been a receptacle for a lot of our postindustrial fears and some deeper, more primal fears, too. Take away the costume and the derring-do, and this guy could be a person, or people, that we know. We know he doesn't exist, but, with just a mental squint or two, we can convince ourselves that he *might*. Comic book publishing has matured to the point that anything that other media do is fair game for comics, and that includes genuine characterization, a look at what's deep under the surface.

Dr. Robin Rosenberg has looked down there, down deep, using the tools of clinical psychology and answered questions about the Batman we know best, the one we can agree on. It's a fascinating examination of a popular character and a witty introduction to Dr. Rosenberg's discipline, eminently readable as either psychology or pop culture and when read as both simultaneously, a treat.

Dennis O'Neil
Nyack, N.Y.
May 2012

ROBIN S. ROSENBERG

ACKNOWLEDGEMENTS

I owe numerous debts of gratitude to the people who helped shaped this book directly and indirectly. First I want to thank the people who have created and shaped Batman over the years, providing such a rich history and psychological tapestry of a character into which I, and others, can explore. In particular, conversations with the following creators have influenced, informed and inspired me: Denny O'Neil, Steve Englehart, Paul Levitz, Jeph Loeb, and Michael Uslan. Thanks for generously sharing your thoughts. Thanks also to Norm Breyfogle for allowing me to use (and adapt) his wonderful illustration on the cover, and to Lillian Laserson for her counsel.

Next, I want to thank my comics scholar friends and colleagues for their support and, most germane to this book, leading me to think ever more deeply about Batman and his world: Peter Coogan, Lawrence Rubin, Travis Langley, Kate Clancy, Randy Duncan, Matthew Smith. Particular thanks go to Andrea Letamendi for her feedback on a draft of this book.

To my colleagues who are mental health clinicians: thanks for reading drafts of the manuscript and supporting me in other ways. This book is far better for your efforts. Specifically, thanks to Andrea Letamendi, Travis Langley, Lawrence Rubin (note that they are also comics scholars!), Robin Apple, Hildy Augustin, Jennifer Dyer-Friedman, and Carol Peyser.

Finally, to my family: Thanks for reading drafts, tolerating dinner conversations about Batman's mental health, and for being my own personal superheroes. Stephen, Neil, David, and Justin: You are my super-team and enrich my world. To Steven, Ben, Keith, and Andy, for being there. And to Bunny and Ed, for being you.

CHAPTER 1

IS THERE A PROBLEM HERE?

What's the matter with Batman? There must be something wrong with him, right? After all, he does things most of us wouldn't do in a million years: He dresses up in a bat costume and puts his life on the line night after night, without any official status. He's a billionaire, yet he dedicates a significant portion of his personal wealth to fund his "hobby" of being a crime fighter. He has no real personal life to speak of—at least not one that isn't directly connected to his work as Batman. (Note, though, that the same can be said of many of us!) He broods, he can be obsessive in his preparations to tangle with criminals, and the fact that he witnessed the murder of his parents must have left a scar. These facets of his life are certainly unusual, but the question I investigate in this book is whether these issues—along with various problems and "symptoms"—place Batman in the "abnormal" range from a mental health perspective. If so, just how bad is his problem (or problems)?

In fact, a fair number of people in our world and in Batman's world have wondered whether something is wrong with him. I sometimes speak at comic conventions and people are fascinated by the question of whether there is something clinically wrong with Batman. Batman is "different" from other people in the world he inhabits, and people wonder about where the line is that separates "different-normal" from "different-abnormal." Although people in our world may not be different in the ways that Batman is (for instance, very, very few of them dress up as a giant bat except at Halloween or comic conventions), his stories can lead us to think about what it takes to be considered "abnormal"—whether he is more than simply different, but rather has a mental illness.

After all, at first glance dressing up like a bat in public (or even in private) would seem to suggest a significant problem. Dr. Chase Meridian, the psychologist in the film *Batman Forever* (1995), is one such person. She remarks "Well, let's just say that I could write a hell of a paper on a grown man who dresses like a flying rodent."

This book is, in a way, the fulfillment of Dr. Meridian's aspiration. It is intended to explore Batman's issues from a psychological perspective—to determine whether his actions, thoughts, and feelings indicate a mental illness.

Evaluating Batman

Let me state clearly at the outset that I'm going to talk about Batman as if he were a real person. You and I both know that he's a fictitious character, but part of what makes him such a compelling character is thinking about what it would be like if he *did* exist, if he were real. So in my discussions about him I'm not generally going to talk about why writers might have written particular stories, added specific characters, or how the Comics Code Authority guidelines might have affected his character, other characters, or the stories. I'm going to take him as he is and try to understand him, contradictions and all.

In the following chapters of this book, part of my

goal is to determine whether Batman's actions and problems reach the level necessary to be diagnosed with any of the disorders in the "psychiatric diagnostic bible" at the time of this writing: *The Diagnostic and Statistical Manual, Fourth Edition-Text Revision*, abbreviated as DSM-IV-TR.* The specific disorders that seem to be the most likely candidates, and will be discussed, include:

- Dissociative Identity Disorder (Chapter 2)
- Depression (Chapter 3)
- Obsessive-Compulsive Disorder (Chapter 4)
- Posttraumatic Stress Disorder (Chapter 5)
- Antisocial Personality Disorder (Chapter 6)

The final chapter (Chapter 7) examines Batman with a broad view of his problems and strengths.

My evaluation of Batman is intended both to entertain and to educate. People familiar with Batman stories may find my views on the Caped Crusader's mental state interesting and illuminating. My hope is that you will also learn something about psychology in the process—something that can be of use to you as you think about yourself or other people.

---

* For brevity's sake, in the rest of the book I'll refer to it simply as DSM-IV. It was published by the American Psychiatric Association in 2000.

Clinical Evaluation: A Continual Process

When mental health clinicians are asked to make a clinical evaluation of someone, they do so by talking to the person being evaluated, observing that person and, in some cases, obtaining information from others—family members, referring doctors, the court, or law enforcement agencies if they are involved. In some cases, psychological or medical testing is done to help clarify a question about the person's functioning, such as whether he or she has delusions (entrenched beliefs that are not based on reality) or whether the person's cognitive functioning is impaired in some way.

I couldn't interview Batman directly (folks dressed as Batman at comic conventions don't count), so how did I evaluate him? My clinical impressions and assessment of Batman are based on the stories that I've read or seen. Just like any mental health clinician, then, my conclusions are based on what I observe and what has been reported to me of the person.

Making my task even more challenging is the sheer number of stories about him: In his many decades of existence, Batman has been featured in an almost countless number of stories in comic books, films, television shows (including cartoon shows), novels, and graphic novels. He's been featured working solo, with various members of his bat-family (e.g., Robin, Nightwing,* Batgirl), and in team-ups with other superheroes, such as Superman. I have not read or seen every story that features Batman. Not even close. So when you read this book, you might find that you disagree with me, based on Batman stories that you know but I've not encountered. Just as mental health clinicians sometimes revise their diagnoses and understanding of a patient when additional information points to symptoms or strengths of which they were previously unaware, I might well revise my conclusions if I knew all of the salient stories.

If you disagree with my conclusions because you know of specific stories that support different conclusions than the ones I reach, please let me know; please send to me the name of the specific story, a brief summary of it, and if possible, the relevant dialogue, narration, or artwork. You can send that information to me at WhatsTheMatterWithBatman@gmail.com. If and when there is enough information to warrant changing my diagnoses and overall evaluation, I'll revise this book in a second edition, credit you in the revised

---

* Nightwing is the codename for adult crimefighter Dick Grayson; when Dick was younger, he was the first Robin, Batman's sidekick. Nightwing is primarily based in Blüdhaven but comes back to Gotham City from time to time to help Batman.

acknowledgement section, and keep you posted.

Let's Get Some Issues Out Of the Way

There are a few aspects of Batman's life that I'd like to address right off the bat (no pun intended): that he dresses up like a bat, that he takes teenage boys as his wards *and sidekicks*, whether he has a substance abuse problem, that he devotes so much money to his life as Batman, and that he has no real personal life. Let's see whether any of these things indicate that something is really wrong with Batman.

Dressing Up

He dresses up like a bat. I grant that it is weird, but the issue at hand is whether it's more than that—whether it's a sign of mental illness. My answer is that in Batman's case it is not, for several reasons. First, Bruce Wayne didn't decide to walk—or swoop—around the streets of Gotham in a bat costume because he actually thought he was a bat. Wayne started dressing as Batman because he had a specific purpose in mind: to disguise his identity when he fought criminals. Sounds like a good idea to me, and one that is used by military personnel when necessary (though not the bat part). Wayne also wanted his disguise to serve another function: to evoke fear in criminals. As Wayne noted to himself in Batman's origin story in 1939: "Criminals are a superstitious cowardly lot... so my disguise must be able to strike terror into their hearts. I must be a creature of the night, black, terrible..."[*] Thus, Wayne intentionally set out to wear a disguise that did more than hide his identity. In this sense, his choice of disguise—of costume—was effective because it met his objectives. Yes, we can argue whether a snake costume would have been more effective, but that would have been harder to squeeze into.

Additionally, Batman's use of his attire is analogous to police officers wearing their uniform, or butlers wearing their uniform, when on duty. Uniforms (of which his costume is one) signal what the wearer's role is. If you see someone in a police uniform, you expect certain kinds of behavior: If the officer pulls a gun and points it at someone running, it will likely mean something different to you then if the gun-holder wasn't wearing that uniform. The uniform immediately conveys context to understand the wearer's behavior.

In a sense, dressing as a bat is akin to dressing as a Ninja or a Navy Seal: the color—black—enables him to hide in the shadows until he wants to emerge, the bats'

---

[*] The story, written by Bill Finger, is in *Detective Comics #33*.

wings enable him to glide short distances, and the overall appearance achieves its ends. It's scary. His willingness to wear this unusual costume (for most of Batman's existence, he wore tights on his legs with "underwear" on the outside, which most people find weird) speaks to his dedication to his mission and how important he thinks the costume is. And, as we see, it is.

In what cases might Wayne's costume be considered a possible indication of mental illness? If Wayne actually believed that he was a bat (that is, if he had delusions), it would certainly suggest a mental illness such as schizophrenia or delusional disorder. If Wayne wore his batsuit for sexual excitement, it might indicate a sexual fetish. Another red flag would arise if Wayne thought he was a different person—a different identity—when he dressed as Batman; if he did, he might be suffering from dissociative identity disorder, discussed in the next chapter. (On a related note, in the book I refer to "Batman" and "Bruce Wayne" somewhat interchangeably, but I typically I refer to him as "Batman" when he's fighting crime or in other ways functioning in his role as the Caped Crusader. I'm more likely to refer to him was "Wayne" when discussing his pre-Batman days or his life as a "regular man" rather than a crime-fighter.)

Why Wards: Taking Youngsters Under His Bat-Wing

Batman has taken five youngsters under his wing to become Robin: Dick Grayson (the original Robin, who as an adult went on to become Nightwing), Jason Todd (who later took the name the Red Hood), Tim Drake (who as an adult went on to become Red Robin), Stephanie Brown (who later became the fifth Batgirl), and Damian Wayne (Bruce's previously unknown son, whose mother is Talia al Ghul—she is the daughter of Ra's al Ghul). It's a curious thing for a romantically unattached man with a dangerous lifestyle to assume legal responsibility for a young teen—as he did with Dick Grayson. Also curious is why he trains and accepts minors as sidekicks in a dangerous profession. Might this be an indication of mental illness on Wayne's part?

To answer that question, we need to understand Wayne's motives. I think his motives were generative.* In this context, the term *generative* comes from Erik Erikson's term *generativity*, which refers to a desire to

---

* Although some people have read sexual motives into Wayne's relationship with Dick Grayson (notably Fredric Wertham in the 1950s), I don't think their relationship had sexual overtones and writers of Batman stories have stated that they wrote Wayne as a heterosexual character without a sexual attraction to Grayson. Their relationship was and is more like that of father and son.

guide and nurture the next generation.* People can be generative in a variety of ways: through formal or informal mentoring at work, creating objects for others to use, or helping to rear children. When Wayne first took in Dick Grayson, I believe he was acting on generative impulses. Grayson's family was part of a circus act and Dick had witnessed his parents' murders, mirroring Bruce Wayne's witnessing his own parents' murders. Wayne took in Grayson to help someone in pain from growing up alone and isolated. He gave Grayson the gift of a mentor that he himself did not have.

Okay so far, but why put a child in danger by taking him to skirmishes with criminals? That's a harder question to answer. Initially when Robin first appeared on the scene in 1940,† the world was a more innocent place and criminals were much less willing to harm law enforcement officers and children. Nonetheless, exposing Dick to danger was a clear lapse in judgment on Wayne's

---

* According to Erik Erickson, generativity is a key challenge to the seventh stage of development and stands in contrast to its opposing tendency of stagnation, a self-centeredness in which the individual doesn't better society in some way. His book on development is Erikson, Erik H. (1959). *Identity and the Life Cycle*. New York: International Universities Press.

† In *Detective Comics #38*; Robin was created by Bob Kane, Bill Finger, and artist Jerry Robinson.

part. A very clear lapse. Wayne might have wanted to help buffer Grayson's loss, but there were many ways he could have done that without putting the youngster directly in harm's way as they battled criminals. For instance, he could have used Grayson as an assistant who stayed in the Batcave, much as Alfred does, and as does the character Oracle, who helps Batman through her work at her command center.[*]

Further lapses in judgment came with his taking on each subsequent Robin. In Jason Todd's case, Wayne struggled against the lesser of two evils; Todd had been trying to steal the Batmobile's hubcaps and Wayne felt that if Todd weren't taken in hand and shaped to use his talents for good then Todd would end up on the wrong side of the law.

Other Robins (Tim Drake and Stephanie Brown) have had that role because they asked Batman to allow them to be Robin. (They were young and the idea of being Robin is exciting and cool, as well as providing a great purpose to their lives.) It's up to the adult—to Batman—to exercise good judgment, which he didn't. It

---

[*] Oracle is Barbara Gordon's codename; Barbara Gordon had originally been Batgirl, but after the Joker shot her at her home she was left without the use of her legs and is wheelchair bound. (Note: The relaunch of the DC Universe in 2011 had Barbara Gordon with full use of her legs and in the role of Batgirl.)

may have been bad judgment for him to accede to their wish and continue to allow them to be in the role, but that doesn't mean Batman has a mental disorder: Bad judgment does not necessarily indicate a psychiatric disorder.

Batman didn't have anything to do with the most recent Robin—Damian Wayne—assuming that role. Wayne didn't even know that he had a son until presented with his pre-teen son Damian.* Damian's ascension to the role of Robin occurred during a period of Wayne's extended absence from Gotham City†, when the adult Dick Grayson stepped into the role of Batman; it was Grayson who allowed Damian to become Robin. Once Bruce Wayne returned, however, he allowed his son to continue in that role.‡ Given that Damian Wayne had been trained at a young age to kill—by the nefarious League of Assassins—it is (somewhat) understandable that Wayne would want to try to remold Damian to use his talents for good, just as Wayne attempted to do with Jason Todd.

Substance Abuse: Pain Relief

---

* In Grant Morrison's story arc *Batman and Son* (1996).

† During the *Final Crisis* storyline in the comics (2008).

‡ In *Batman & Robin #2* (2011).

Batman's crime-fighting activities can leave his body battered, bruised, or broken. Alfred not only acts as butler to Bruce Wayne and concierge to Batman, he also acts as doctor and nurse to the Caped Crusader— stitching wounds, setting broken bones, even performing some surgical procedures. Batman's body suffers.

Does Batman take pain medication to help him keep going, and if so, is he "addicted"—does he have a substance abuse problem? Stories don't often indicate that Batman takes anything to dull his pain, probably because if he did he'd be slowed down and his senses dulled—and make him more likely to get *really* hurt by a criminal. So it's not likely that he self-medicates. Most of the time that he's had a significant injury he seems to do what some people with chronic pain have learned to do: accept the pain, compartmentalize it, and live life anyway.

All That Money

Wayne is an incredibly smart man who has found a way to make his money grow, and then to divert money to fund his activities as Batman. I don't see anything about his spending habits that indicates signs of a mental illness. It would be a warning sign if he went on spending sprees and he often purchased unneeded items—this could possibly indicate manic episodes of bipolar disorder.[*] Or if Bruce spent large sums of money to protect himself against an unknown enemy that no one else had reason to believe posed a threat—this could indicate that Wayne might be suffering from paranoia. But that's not the case. The money he spends to support his activities as Batman, phenomenal though they may be, is well spent to prepare him to fight Gotham City's criminals.

What Personal Life?

Bruce Wayne doesn't have much of a personal life. When he's not busy as Batman (in or out of the cowl), he's overseeing the Wayne Foundation (his philanthropic organization) or Wayne Enterprises (formerly called WayneCorp, the company he owns and from which his wealth derives). Moreover, he must devote some time to the parties of the rich and famous (including his own) to keep up his billionaire-playboy façade. He's juggling multiple full-time jobs. Yes, he tends not to have relationships with people outside of

---

[*] One could argue that among the wealthy, most purchases are "unneeded": another house or apartment, another sports car, another work of art, clothes for a makeover. Such spending sprees might indicate mania if they were different from the person's usual behavior, and occurred along with other symptoms of mania.

his work life, but the same can be said for many of us—particularly if we spend many hours at work, side by side with our colleagues. Plus, given the secret of the Batman part of his life, it's hard to let other people in. If and when he does tell a woman he's romantically involved with about his secret life, she's likely to get twisted up when he goes to work each night.

This is what happened with Silver St. Cloud; she is a wealthy and sharp woman in Bruce's circle who deduced that Bruce Wayne is also Batman. Although they love each other, after she witnessed the Caped Crusader fight the Joker she realized that she couldn't be in a romantic relationship because of the stress of worrying whether he'll come home each night.[*] One appeal of Catwoman as a romantic partner is that there's less that Wayne has to keep from her (except his Wayne identity in some stories), and she truly understands who he is as Batman. He is fully known.

Bruce is also fully known by his butler/sidekick Alfred. Ditto with any of the five Robins. Alfred and each Robin know about Bruce's dual identities, about his history and vulnerabilities, and about his mission.

---

[*] The seminal story of Silver and Bruce, written by Steve Englehart in 1977-1978, is in *Detective Comics #469-476, 478, 479*, and also collected in the bound volume *Batman: Strange Apparitions*.

Wayne is thus truly and fully known and accepted by more people than most of us can claim.*

Now that we've discussed various aspects of Wayne's poor judgment (Robins), good judgment (costume, financial allocations, use of natural pain management techniques), and other quirks, let's turn to the types of mental disorders that seem most relevant as possible diagnoses. I start with a discussion of his alter ego.

---

* As I have noted in other writings, one element of his personal life that I find potentially psychologically interesting is his relationship with Alfred Pennyworth, his butler. In Wayne's youth, Alfred functioned as a de facto guardian, yet during Wayne's adulthood, Alfred's role is that of assistant: he takes orders from Wayne, but their familiarity and long history allows Alfred to "reprimand" Wayne occasionally. The closest analogies I can think of is the relationship between an adult and his or her nanny from childhood, or an executive and his or her coach.

CHAPTER 2

DISSOCIATIVE IDENTITY DISORDER?

Bruce Wayne is the Batman. The Batman is Bruce Wayne. He answers to both names, but sometimes talks about his other "self" in the third person. When he's walking the halls of Wayne Manor or his apartment in Wayne Towers, in his thought bubbles (or in his conversations with Alfred) Wayne talks about Batman as if the Caped Crusader were a different person. He has a dual identity, but does he also have an identity disorder?

Alter Ego/Dual Identity

Many superheroes—in fact, *most* superheroes—have dual identities. Clark Kent/Superman, Diana Prince/Wonder Woman, Peter Parker/Spider-Man, and so on. Given the nature of the work that superheroes do, of course they want to protect their "civilian" identities, just as covert operatives and undercover police officers do. Other people live dual lives, such as certain people who are gay, lesbian, intersex* and are also "in the closet." Moreover, like superheroes, undercover agents and people in the closet may have dual identities, using different names for each identity.

In fact many of us have dual or multiple identities, particularly if we consider our online lives: we may have different and distinct identities as bloggers, as gamers, on Facebook or Twitter, or when posting a comment. In fact, being anonymous is an identity. The internet isn't the only mechanism for eliciting an alter ego—a term that refers to the "other" identity. Even before the internet, each of us had multiple identities,

---

* The term *intersex* refers to people who were born with sexual or reproductive anatomy that does not fall into the typical categories of male or female. Examples include people who appear mostly female but have a significantly large clitoris, or people who appear mostly male but have a significantly small penis (see www.isna.org for more information).

although most of the time each identity didn't have a distinct name.

What I mean by the term *dual identities* is that a person has two different ways of "being" when with other people, two different names, and two apparently distinctly different sets of personality traits. I say "apparently" because all of us behave differently when with different sets of people and so might appear to have different sets of personality traits in different contexts.

For instance, who you are when you're with your parents is different (at least somewhat) than who you are when you're with children. Who you are when you're with your boss is different than who you are when you are with your best friend. Each version of you might be representative of "you," but how you see yourself, how you act, even how you feel, will likely be somewhat different depending on the social context. We still have a coherent sense of self across the different contexts we find ourselves in and we have memories of our experiences in each of the identities. Having a dual identity, or even multiple identities, isn't necessarily a problem.

Batman's dual identity, however, isn't quite like ours. He sometimes talks about himself—to himself—in the third person. In fact, even when he's dressed as

Batman he sometimes talks about himself as Batman in the third person: "They say **The Batman** can solve **anything**—but he's up a stump on this one!"[*] (emphasis in original). In fact, Batman has a third identity he uses from time to time, that of Matches Malone. Matches was originally a crook who died, but Batman has perpetuated Malone's existence by impersonating him occasionally in order to infiltrate the criminal underworld in Gotham. (Batman also has other aliases under which he operates.)

Is Batman confused about who he is—about his identity? *Identity problems*, in the psychiatric sense, are conceived of as pathological symptoms of dissociation— a separation of mental processes that are normally integrated, such as those of perception, memory, and self-awareness. For mental health clinicians, most frequently if someone has an "identity problem" it means either that the person isn't sure who he or she is— name, profession, family members—or else the person might assume a new identity. Thus, if Batman had an identity problem of this type, then either:

- Bruce Wayne wouldn't be sure who he is (that is, he wouldn't know that he's a billionaire playboy-philanthropist), or

---

[*] In "The Laughing Fish," *Detective Comics #475* (1978).

- he would assume a new identity—full time. He wouldn't switch between assuming the personas of Bruce Wayne and of the Batman.

What about the disorder that is colloquially known as *multiple personality disorder*? In DSM-IV,[*] the edition of the "diagnostic bible" of mental illness at the time this book was published, this disorder is known as *dissociative identity disorder*. In order to determine whether Batman has dissociative identity disorder, we first have to know about the disorder itself and what it takes to get diagnosed with this disorder.

What IS Dissociative Identity Disorder?

The hallmark of dissociative identity disorder (DID) is a rupture in the normally integrated sense of self and memory of personal events. Specifically, the diagnosis of DID requires the presence of at least two distinct personality states or identities, and personal memories of each personality state are not necessarily accessible to the others. I'll unpack this definition and then see whether it applies to Wayne.

---

[*] As noted in the previous chapter, DSM-IV stands for *Diagnostic and Statistical Manual, 4th edition*.

Personality States, A.K.A. Alters

Each personality state is sometimes referred to as an *alter,* and has its own stable way of thinking about and relating to itself, other people, and the environment. What is intended by the term *distinct personality state* is that when in a given personality state, the individual temporarily seems to become a different person. For instance, a given alter has different likes and dislikes compared to his other alters, and he responds to the environment in different ways. Distinct personality states may each have their own names.

Who's In Control?

To be diagnosed with dissociative identity disorder, at least two of the alters must alternate "controlling" the person's behavior repeatedly—the person changes his or her behavior in ways consistent with the alter's identity. When an alter of a young boy is present, for instance, the person's voice and mannerisms will resemble that of a young boy. Thus, an alter or personality state isn't simply having an alter ego with a different name, set of clothes, occupation, and different friends; it is about a fundamental shift in preferences and behaviors for the time period during which the alter is dominant.

Memory Gaps: What Happened?

Another criterion for a diagnosis of DID is that the person has significant gaps in personal memory because he or she is unable to remember events that transpired when one or more other alters was in control. The person may not remember what he or she did yesterday afternoon, or how a brand new coat never seen before ended up in the closet. When one personality state recedes and another comes to the fore, it can seem as if the person was waking up from sleep, with no memory of how he or she got into the current situation. Friends or family members may recount events that the individual simply doesn't remember (because another alter was "in control" during the events).* Some caveats:

---

* The diagnosis of DID is controversial, and there are two general models about how the symptoms arise. According to the posttraumatic model, people who have experienced severe and chronic abuse since a young age dissociate while they are being abused or otherwise traumatized. Over time, the dissociated experiences become a different identity. In contrast, the sociocognitive model suggests that DID is the result of the therapist's inadvertently causing the patient to act in ways that are consistent with DID through the questions the patient is asked and the attention the therapist (and others) pay to answers consistent with DID; suggestible patients (who may have been abused as children, and who may also have read about or watched films about DID) unconsciously develop distinct identities. For more on this topic and controversy, I suggest you read the chapter on DID in *Science and Pseudoscience in Clinical Psychology* (2004) by Scott Lilienfeld, Steven Lynn, and Jeffrey Lohr, published by Guilford Press.

These gaps in memory must be more than common forgetfulness, and must not be known to arise from substance use or abuse or from a medical illness, such as a brain tumor.

An alter, as outlined in DSM-IV, is thus significantly different than the "different identities" that most people try on when they are in new situations. "Billy" from high school becomes "Will" or "William" when he arrives at college or starts his new job, and he may wear different clothes or hang out with different types of friends. This trying on of "identities" is a common and normal part of getting older and of being in new or different circumstances. But he is the same person, with an integrated sense of self and memories, by whatever name he is called.

Does Batman Have Alters That Take Control?

Bruce Wayne and Batman are clearly different identities in the sense that Batman is a crimefighter and Bruce Wayne is a billionaire playboy, but are they alters? No. Batman reacts as Batman whether he wearing cape and cowl or tuxedo. If there's something bad going down, his impulse to intervene is the same no matter whether he's being Wayne or the Bat. Although his billionaire playboy image is at odds with his Batman identity, the playboy image is simply that—a projected image, a persona. It's not a real identity in the psychological sense of the word; it's not how he sees himself. It's a "cover," much like the cover of a covert operative or undercover detective—he or she can walk the walk and talk the talk, but it's an act. At a charity ball, Bruce can look and act like a playboy, but he never believes himself actually to be one.

He is well aware that his Batman persona protects his civilian identity as Bruce Wayne. For the most part this persona allows him not to worry that his friends will be kidnapped or threatened in an attempt to blackmail or dissuade him from apprehending criminals. As he notes in *Detective Comics #475* (1978), after suspecting that Wayne's girlfriend Silver St. Cloud knows both of his identities he thinks to himself,

> I'm in love with that girl—the real me,
> underneath all the masks! And still, the man
> beneath the mask can't be carelessly revealed!
> My secrets are my protection from death!

Furthermore, the Bruce Wayne and Batman personalities don't alternate control of behavior. His core personality (whatever name is most appropriate—Bruce Wayne or Batman) is always in control, sometimes acting as a playboy, sometimes acting as a frightening crime fighter. His two identities are well thought out, purposeful, and help him fight crime while deflecting any suspicion from his legal identity. As he notes,[*]

> I made a promise on the grave of my parents that I would rid this city of the evil that took their lives. By day, I am Bruce Wayne, billionaire philanthropist. At night, criminals, a cowardly and superstitious lot, call me... Batman.

If he had dissociative identity disorder, he'd react differently when he is the Batman than when he is Bruce Wayne.[†] But Bruce Wayne and the Batman have a unified personality: they think the same, react the same, and have access to the same memories. There are no gaps in memory when he is Bruce versus Batman.

The Take Home Message: Does Batman Have Dissociative Identity Disorder?

---

[*] From Jeph Loeb's *Hush* story (2002-2003).

[†] In case you're wondering whether DID applies to Superman/Clark Kent, the answer is "no." Clark may respond in a cowardly manner and flee a dangerous situation whereas Superman rushes toward the danger, but the former is an act in order to preserve Kent's cover and allow Superman to make his entrance.

Based on my assessment, Wayne doesn't have dissociative identity disorder. Yet at first glance it can seem that having such completely different alter egos is definitely high on the weirdness meter. Think again; dual identities aren't just in fiction. As I noted earlier, many people have dual lives, if less flamboyantly and exaggeratedly than Wayne. Individuals who are homosexuals in the closet live a dual existence: one self is public and one self is private, known only to a select few. An extreme example of this type is that of people who profess one attitude and privately subscribe to or behave in an opposite manner. Examples include publically anti-gay politicians and leaders who were secretly homosexual: Pastor Ted Haggard, former Young Republican National Federation President Glenn Murphy Jr., former California state Senator Roy Ashburn, former Spokane Mayor Jim West.

The concept of dual identities that is expressed by Bruce Wayne/Batman is an exaggeration of an everyday phenomenon experienced by all of us, and isn't so weird after all. It certainly doesn't indicate dissociative identity disorder. But this is not to say that Batman is out of the psychiatric woods yet. He might have several other disorders, and we consider some more in the following chapter.

CHAPTER 3

DEPRESSED?

Bruce Wayne, whether in or out of the cowl, is not a guy who laughs a lot. If, as Bruce Wayne, he's the life of the party, it's because he's acting the part. He doesn't seem to get too much enjoyment from life and it can seem like he spends too much time ruminating—mulling things over (and over and over)—or just simply brooding. Maybe he's depressed. Not just "down," but clinically, diagnosably depressed.

To figure out whether Wayne is depressed, let's first examine the criteria for depression according to the fourth edition of the *Diagnostic and Statistical Manual: DSM-IV*. Depression, or *major depression* as it is technically called, is a diagnosis that rests on nine symptoms, which can be organized into three categories. You can easily remember these categories by the initials ABC: *affect, behavior, cognition*. The symptoms must last at least two weeks; when symptoms last continuously for more than two years, it is considered to be chronic. Let's see what the symptoms are and whether they fit Bruce Wayne.

Affect

Affect is the technical term for emotion, and the diagnosis of depression must include at least one of two emotional symptoms for most days within a two-week period:

1) *depressed mood*. This could be based on Wayne's own view of his mood (if Wayne says he's depressed) or based on the observations of others. For instance, if Alfred found that Wayne was frequently tearful or seemed to be profoundly down in the dumps, his observations might lead a mental health clinician to consider that Wayne had depressed mood.

2) *a significant loss of pleasure or interest in activities*

(technically referred to as *anhedonia*, from the Greek roots *an-*, which means without, and *hedone*, related to pleasure). People with this symptom find that things that used to be enjoyable are no longer so. In fact, people who are depressed find very little to be interesting or enjoyable.

Does Wayne have either or both of these affective symptoms of depression? If you were to ask Wayne whether he's depressed, what do you think he'd say? My guess is that he'd say something to the effect that he's a man with a mission—a difficult mission—and that he doesn't have time to be depressed.

Of course he *could* be depressed but "in denial"; however, if so, other people in his life would probably notice his depressed mood. Does he appear depressed to others? Would Alfred, who knows Wayne better than anyone, think that Bruce was depressed? My bet is that Alfred would concede that Master Wayne isn't the happiest of fellows, and certainly not among the light-hearted, that his mood is what it has been for almost the entirety of Wayne's adult life, but not depressed.

As to the second symptom—a loss of interest or pleasure—it doesn't seem to apply. Batman *is* interested in things and takes pleasure in those things. It's just that most of those activities are unusual, such as developing a new bat-weapon, tracking down a villain, figuring out a villain's nefarious plan or apprehending said villain. Some of his interests are more common, and many of us can relate to them: Driving a responsive car at high speeds; the pursuit of excellence; the deep pleasure of helping other people (though in his case that involves putting villains behind bars or into Arkham Asylum); and the profound sense of satisfaction that comes from doing what you believe in.

Some mental health clinicians might consider Wayne to have the second symptom—anhedonia. Such a clinician might point to the fact that Wayne generally seems to go through the motions of his life, apprehending the bad guys and attending charity balls. He at times seems to force himself to do it, just like other people with depression force themselves to get up in the morning and get dressed.

Although Wayne may have to force himself to go through some of the motions of being (or acting) the billionaire playboy role, his hesitancy to act that role arises because he'd rather spend his time doing things directly related to his job as Batman. Activities interest him, but those activities are very specific and are related to his work as the Caped Crusader. We can think of him as a guy who doesn't like his "day job" (as billionaire playboy) much, and can't wait to get off the job so he can engage in his other activities—the ones that interest him. He isn't considered depressed simply because he doesn't like his day job and "lives" for his life outside of work. (Think of an artist or musician who has works a job to pay the bills, but who really comes alive later, when creating his or her art.)

Although Wayne might not be interested in seeing the latest talked-about film or going to the hot new restaurant that's opening in Gotham City, his lack of interest or pleasure in *these* activities doesn't mean he has anhedonia. He's only interested in such things if he thought they would somehow help him in his job as Batman. Does Wayne have either affective symptoms of depression? I say no.

Behavioral and Physical Symptoms

Among the symptoms of depression are three that involve specific behaviors and changes in aspects of physical functioning. The symptoms are changes in weight and appetite, sleep, and motor activity. These symptoms must occur most days within a two-week period.

Change in Appetite or Weight

One behavioral sign of depression is a *significant change in appetite or weight* that isn't because of an intentional change in diet or food intake. (Batman on a diet?) Does this symptom apply to Wayne? He may have days or even weeks when he's so preoccupied with catching villains that he's not hungry. In fact there have been many a time when Alfred brings a tray of food to the Batcave because Batman is so consumed with his work. But having no appetite because of being preoccupied with a task (or consumed by it, in his case) isn't the same as having no appetite because of being depressed.

What about weight change? His weight has been remarkably stable over the decades, except for weight increases related to his bulked up muscle. Such weight gains are intentional. He must've increased his exercise intensity to bulk up like that (but could he be taking steroids? He's obsessed enough to be willing to take the medical risks—but, as of this writing, such behavior would not reflect a mental illness).

This symptom clearly doesn't apply to Batman.

Change in Sleep: A Tired Batman

Another behavioral symptom is *significant changes in sleep* most nights: insomnia (difficulty getting to sleep or staying asleep) or sleeping a lot (called *hypersomnia*). Such changes in sleep can be one of the first symptoms of depression to emerge. Because Batman works nights, Wayne must try to sleep as late in the morning as possible. But the demands of being a figurehead for Wayne Enterprises and running Wayne Foundation require occasional morning appearances; more than likely, he's sleep deprived. This is not a "sleep problem" that arises as part of depression. (In fact, his sleep debt— that is, the accumulated need for sleep—is probably big enough that it could make him seem to have some symptoms of depression when he's just chronically tired!)

Given his level of daily physical challenge and his sleep debt, he probably falls asleep soon after his head hits the pillow. If he has insomnia or hypersomnia (that isn't making up for a sleep debt), there's not much evidence of it.

Change in Psychomotor Activity

The final behavioral symptom is a change in the speed and type of motor activity, specifically either *psychomotor retardation* or *psychomotor agitation*. Psychomotor retardation refers to a general slowing of movements; depressed people with this symptom will take longer to walk across the room, get up from the chair, or answer a question. They feel a deep sense of fatigue that is not relieved by sleep. Typically they make less eye contact, speak more quietly and say less than they do in their previous, non-depressed state.[1]

Psychomotor retardation doesn't appear to be a problem for Batman. If he took much longer to walk across the room than usual, I'd assume he was injured and in pain or else scoping out the situation. Or else he was thinking deep thoughts and preoccupied. Sometimes, as Batman, he may stand still for longer than most people, but that's likely to happen when he's in the shadows, watching his enemies and sizing them up, not because of depression. I grant you that Batman doesn't speak much, but that's part of his persona. He uses silence and pauses to throw off villains. I haven't seen evidence of psychomotor slowing in Batman.

In contrast to psychomotor slowing, psychomotor agitation refers to difficulty sitting still; people with this depressive symptom may pace, fidget, or rub their skin or objects. In essence, they feel agitated and thus compelled to move, even when "at rest." Does Wayne exhibit psychomotor agitation? He might appear restless when he's stuck in a situation as Bruce Wayne while he's needed elsewhere as Batman. He might jiggle his leg, repeatedly check his watch, or play with his cufflinks. He'd be agitated, but it wouldn't be the agitation of depression. It would be the agitation that can arise, appropriately, from urgency and emergencies.

I don't think Bruce Wayne exhibits any of the behavioral symptoms of depression.

Cognition

Cognitive symptoms of depression refer to those that involve changes in the contents of people's thoughts (what they think about) as well as changes in their thought processes (the way they think). The following three symptoms fall under this category, and must occur most days in a two-week span: guilt or sense of worthlessness, problems concentrating or making decisions, and frequent thoughts about dying or suicide.

Guilt or Sense of Worthlessness

People who are depressed may feel *guilty or a sense of worthlessness* that is inappropriate or disproportionate to the situation. For instance, the depressed person may feel guilty about arriving late to work because of a stalled train—which clearly isn't his or her fault. People with this symptom often brood over their past mistakes, blaming themselves and in turn deepening their depression.

It's important to make a distinction between "appropriate" guilt and guilt that is disproportional or inappropriate to the situation. People who are depressed are prone to feel guilty for most anything negative that happens. They attribute such events to themselves, even when that clearly is not the case. It's as if people who are depressed feel so badly about themselves that they wrongfully attribute the "down" parts of life's vicissitudes as being caused by their perceived badness or unworthiness.

Guilt About Parents' Deaths

Bruce Wayne is certainly a man who carries a sense of guilt. Guilt that he survived the bloodbath of his parents' murder in the alley. Guilt for the role he played—real or perceived—in his family's walk down the dark alley the fateful evening of their murder. The guilt is laid on most thickly in the film *Batman Begins,* which implicitly places part of the bad luck of Thomas and Martha Wayne's deaths at young Bruce's feet: Bruce experiences panic while attending an opera performance, so he and his parents leave the performance early and enter the almost-deserted fateful alley where they encounter their murderer. On a rational level as an adult, though, Bruce recognizes that he's not responsible for his parents' deaths. As Wayne says to Ra's al Ghul, in the film *Batman Begins*, when asked whether he feels responsible for his parents' deaths, "My anger outweighs my guilt."

Wayne may still carry around a sense of guilt about his parents' murder, despite his rational understanding that he wasn't responsible for their deaths, but his burden of guilt doesn't seem to resemble the *pervasive* sense of guilt that can be a part of depression.

Guilt About Jason Todd's Death at the Hands of the Joker

In addition to the guilt from this pivotal childhood event, more recently the Batman feels guilty about the death of Jason Todd, the second Robin, at the hands of the Joker. Jason Todd's murder is a seminal event.[*] Here's the basic story: Teenager Jason Todd has been behaving too recklessly and Batman grounds him from acting as Robin for a while. Unbeknownst to Batman, Todd then goes off to find his biological mother,

---

[*] His murder takes place in the story "A Death in the Family" (*Batman #426-429*, 1988-1989), and a variant of it is recounted in the cartoon film *Batman: Under the Red Hood* (2010).

whom Todd only recently discovered was not the woman who raised him. On Todd's quest, he ends up crossing paths with the Joker; the villain beats Todd mercilessly, ties him up and sets a bomb to go off in the room. Todd dies soon after the bomb explodes.

Even though Todd's death comes at the hands of the Joker, Bruce Wayne feels guilty about it for many reasons. He feels guilty for taking Todd in and training him to be Robin. Wayne also feels guilty for not doing a better job of molding Todd—to dampen the boy's impulsivity and recklessness. (In fact, it is because Todd was impulsive that he ended up crossing paths with the Joker alone.)

An additional reason Wayne feels guilty is that he wasn't there to stop what happened. Batman was out on another mission and didn't even know that the Joker and Robin would be on the same continent (neither was in the U.S. at the time). Batman carries this collective sense of guilt for years and over many storylines. His guilt is not dissimilar to that of soldiers, police officers, and firefighters, among others, who live with guilt when they weren't able to save a colleague. It is always there, but lessens with time.

Like many a busy parent juggling multiple obligations, Batman did not feel he could afford to spend more time with Jason to understand better what Jason was going through. Jason was angry and rebellious and at the time it was easy for Wayne to rationalize that Batman's time would be better spent chasing villains than trying to connect with this teen who just wanted to be left alone anyway.

In my opinion, Batman's ongoing guilt is not excessive or disproportional. Wayne *did* take in Todd, Wayne *didn't* mold Todd as assiduously as he did the first Robin (Dick Grayson), and Wayne *did* leave Todd to his own devices when the teen was grounded. Given the way events unfolded, Batman's feeling profoundly guilty about Todd's death is understandable. Batman's guilt is appropriate to the context. (It is, therefore, perhaps a tad odd that Batman goes on to take more wards and place them in similar situations, but that is a separate issue.) Despite Wayne's guilt, though, it doesn't generally interfere with his ability to do his job; his guilt doesn't lead to impaired functioning or significant distress that is inappropriate to the situation.

Worthlessness?

Some people who are depressed feel worthless, feel that they are "bad," don't deserve any good things that come, and even that they deserve whatever bad things life dishes out. Wayne does *not* seem to have a sense of worthlessness. Yes, he has periods of self-doubt and wonders whether he's doing a good-enough job as Batman. Invariably, he continues his work. He knows that as Wayne he can "do good" through his foundation, and that as Batman his life, his mission, and his purpose are very worthwhile.

Sometimes he even wonders whether he "deserves" to have an intimate, lasting relationship with a woman. But that's because his role as Batman takes up so much space in his life and is so fraught with danger. Thus, his questions about deserving a relationship aren't because he feels "unworthy." Rather, they're based on his past experience of how hard his life as Batman is on a romantic relationship, which he learned from his relationship with Silver St. Cloud (among others).

Problems Concentrating, Making Decisions: An Indecisive Batman?

Another type of cognitive symptom involves *difficulty concentrating, making decisions, or thinking as clearly as usual.* This symptom may be noticed by others or by the depressed person. Bruce Wayne does *not* have these problems with thinking; if anything, he's an über-thinker. He displays a phenomenal ability to concentrate, except on the rare occasions he's suffering the temporary after-effects of a concussion or drug (not taken voluntarily! He's not a substance abuser—at least not yet). Moreover, he doesn't have any difficulty making decisions, either in the part of his life as Bruce Wayne, or in the part of his life as Batman. In fact, when acting as Batman, he habitually seeks out adequate information upon which to base a decision, then makes it.

In contrast, people with depression can find the process—and responsibility—of making a decision overwhelming. In some cases, making a decision, even about what to wear, can seem to require too much mental effort. In other cases, the responsibility a depressed person feels about possibly making a wrong decision is too heavy a burden to bear, even for non-weighty decisions such as what movie to see with friends. This aspect of depression is far from the decisive Bruce Wayne/Batman that we see in print, film, and television. Rarely does Batman experience self-doubt except when significant setbacks in his fight against crime prompt appropriate self-reflection—and also after Todd's death.

Frequent Thoughts about Dying or Suicide: Contemplating Death

The final cognitive symptom of depression is *frequent thoughts about dying or about suicide*, though not necessarily with a specific plan or actual attempt. I see no signs that Wayne has this cognitive symptom. Yes, he does sometimes think about death (although not suicide), but that's appropriate for his chosen career path. Someone in the military who frequently experiences combat or dangerous situations may think of death regularly. Ditto for police officers or firefighters, whose lives are significantly at risk on a daily or weekly basis.

In contrast, people who are depressed and exhibit this symptom may think about death or suicide recurrently in one of two ways: either viewing death as a release from how persistently awful they feel or as an appropriate end because they feel unworthy to live. In the former case, in which death is a release, the weight of all the depressive symptoms feels like too much to bear. They don't experience enough pleasure in living or have a strong enough reason to live to offset the pain and effort they feel chronically. When depressed, people can feel that they're a drain on friends and family, and wonder whether the friends and family in their lives would be better off if they died. People with this cognitive symptom aren't necessarily suicidal, but they think about death in a positive, or at least neutral, light. Others with depression explicitly think about killing themselves. They may go so far as to develop a plan of how they'd do it. These descriptions of depressed people don't sound like Batman.

To summarize, I don't think that Batman has any cognitive symptoms of depression. That said, I agree that a case could be made that he has excessive guilt. Although I don't think that his guilt is disproportionate—and therefore his guilt isn't a symptom of depression—other mental health clinicians might disagree. (Such disagreement isn't uncommon in clinical cases that are not clear-cut.) A clinician's own background, experience with certain types of problems, and other factors can nudge that line in one direction or another. Moreover, each clinician must decide whether symptoms of depression—or of any psychiatric disorder—cause *significant enough* distress, create *significant enough* dysfunction, or lead to *significant enough* risk of harm.

Depressed Enough?

Let's say, for argument's sake, that you've submitted information to me that convinced me that he's got one or two symptoms of depression. Having a symptom or two of depression doesn't mean that the person is depressed. In fact, DSM-IV specifies that to be diagnosed with depression, an individual must have experienced five or more of the nine symptoms, and at least one of the symptoms must be an affective symptom—depressed mood or loss of pleasure or interests. Moreover, the symptoms must occur most of the day, on most days, for at least two weeks; and the symptoms must represent a *change* from the person's normal functioning.

There's an additional hurdle for the symptoms to merit a diagnosis of major depression: The symptoms must also impair the person's functioning in some way, either at work or socially (with family, for instance), or cause significant distress. In Batman's case, this hurdle means that he must be sufficiently depressed so as to be unable to don the cowl, to mentor Robin or to carry out his duties as head of Wayne Foundation. Or, Batman could attempt these tasks but do them poorly because of depression. (Alternatively, depressive symptoms could create a significant risk of harm—such as a suicide attempt—but this isn't the case with Batman. Whatever risk of harm he encounters it is *not* because of depression, but because he chooses to put himself in harm's way in order to apprehend criminals.)

Is Wayne clinically depressed? No. Whatever

"symptoms" he has (e.g., guilt, seeming paucity of pleasure) are better understood as arising from his experiences, his dedication to a very serious mission, and his general temperament as someone who is not a spontaneous, fun-loving guy. And even if he did have at least five symptoms, his functioning isn't impaired, at least not by depression. Yes, when his back was broken[*] he was sidelined and he understandably felt helpless, dejected, and worthless as Batman while he was out of commission. But generally speaking, Batman is a long way from being clinically depressed.

What About Dysthymic Disorder?

Let's say that readers send in enough relevant Batman stories to convince me that his guilt is excessive, that he's sad, that he has anhedonia, *and* that his functioning is impaired—at least in the domain of relationships. He still would only have three depressive symptoms, not the necessary minimum number of five. Wayne's three symptoms might meet the criteria for a less intense, but longer-lasting mood disorder called *dysthymic disorder*.

To be diagnosed with this disorder, the person must have depressed mood and at least two other

---

[*] By Bane in *Batman #497* (1993).

symptoms for at least two years. The depressive symptoms of dysthymia are thus, by definition, chronic. By virtue of being chronic, people with this disorder typically think of themselves—their character, their personality—in depressed ways, and they may not remember a time when they were different. They may see themselves as bad company, not fun to be with, undeserving of good friends and family. This is just how they are. In contrast, people with major depression—even when the episode of depression lasts a long time—remember that depression is not their "usual" state. They want to go back to how they were before they were depressed.*

Thus, if Wayne had the three symptoms I mentioned earlier (and clinically significant distress or impaired functioning), he could be diagnosed with dysthymic disorder. However, I don't think he even has three symptoms, so dysthymic disorder doesn't fit.

Okay, Bruce Wayne isn't clinically depressed,

---

* Major depression is much more common than dysthymic disorder; among American adults, 16.5% will be diagnosed with the former disorder in their lifetimes, whereas only 2.5% will be diagnosed with dysthymic disorder, as noted in Kessler, R. C., Berglund, P. A., Demler, O., Jin, R., & Walters, E. E. (2005). Lifetime prevalence and age-of-onset distributions of DSM-IV disorders in the National Comorbidity Survey Replication (NCS-R). *Archives of General Psychiatry, 62*, 593-602.

either with major depression or dysthymia. Given his life and the work he does, why isn't he depressed? What protects him from depression?

Why He Isn't Depressed: Risk and Protective Factors Associated With Depression

Bruce Wayne has experienced numerous stressors that would send many people into depression: witnessing the death of his parents; losing his parents at a young age; the loss of and his guilt about Jason Todd. Add to that his continual, endless battle against the villains who inhabit Gotham City. In this context, it's remarkable that Wayne hasn't gotten depressed. Why hasn't he? In order to answer that question, let's examine known risk factors or variables associated with depression and determine which—if any—risk factors and protective factors he has.

Family History of Depression: Depressed Waynes?

People with a family history of depression are more likely to experience depression themselves, in part because of a genetic vulnerability and in part because some of the behaviors that a depressed parent inadvertently exhibits can makes the children—even when they become adults—more vulnerable to depression.[2] For instance, depressed parents may, because of their depression, pay less attention to their child or be more critical of the child.[*] From the little that we know of Wayne's upbringing with his parents[†] we have no evidence that either of Wayne's parents battled depression.

A Sense of Agency Versus a Bleak Vision

Some people have ways of thinking about themselves that lead them to be more vulnerable to depression: They have negative views about themselves, the world, and the future. This is referred to as the *negative triad of depression*.[3] For instance, someone with this set of views might feel unlovable or incompetent (view of self), may feel that life is a trial to get through (view of the world) and that things won't get any better (view of the future). Notice that this view makes it hard to look forward to the future since it's forecast to be negative. The negative triad can easily make people feel helpless: No matter what they do, things won't improve (and they don't feel that they deserve things to improve

---

[*] Myrna Weissman and colleagues have researched the topic of depression across generations. Please see Endnote #9 for one reference to this large study.

[†] One such portrayal of his parents is in the film *Batman Begins* (2005).

anyway), so why bother. This outlook would make most people depressed!

One way that Wayne may be protected from getting depressed is that he doesn't have this negative triad. Yes, he may have a negative view of the world (I think a more accurate term would be a cynical view of the world), but he does not usually have a negative view of himself or the world in general—only the part in which villains inhabit. Wayne recognizes that he can and does make things happen, both as the billionaire head of Wayne Enterprises and as Batman. He has a sense of *self-efficacy*, which is the belief that you can do what you set out to do. And he does! In addition, his physical prowess and skill can only add a sense of competence. Consider his thoughts when he's, of all things, buried in a coffin, strapped into a straightjacket. He's been musing about how he has always escaped from previous death traps— dozens of times. But,

> Benchpressing a pine coffin lid through 600 pounds of loose soil that's filling your mouth, crushing your lungs flat and shredding your dehydrated muscles? That's harder.

Yet he is able to escape. After he's free, he adds,

But far from impossible.*

Most of the time, Wayne believes he—and only he—can do something to reduce crime in Gotham, and so his sense of self-efficacy again protects him from this depression-inducing way of thinking. But should the day come when he feels that no matter what he does he can't make a significant dent, he might well get depressed. (His belief that only he can protect Gotham from its most dastardly villains also makes it difficult for him to have a joy-filled, carefree life, but he might not be capable of that even if he stopped wearing the cowl.)

Attributional Style: Why Negative Things Happen

Some people attribute negative events to enduring aspects of themselves (that is, they blame aspects of their personality); such people are more likely to become depressed than are those who attribute negative events to external causes or to situational factors.[4] *Depressive attributional* style is the name given to the tendency to make this type of general attribution to core aspects of oneself (e.g., "this is my fault because I am a _____ person; it's not just this situation or that I'm

---

* From *Batman #681*, part of Grant Morrison's *Batman R.I.P.* storyline (2008).

tired").

This relationship between attributing blame and a tendency toward depression makes sense: Suppose the Joker breaks into a bank and kills hostages. If Batman later blames himself ("I should have predicted Joker's actions, I should have been prepared"), it's a much heavier mental burden to bear than if he blamed external factors. An example of the latter might be: "The Joker is unpredictable and ruthless." Research reveals that people who have an enduring depressive attribution style are more likely to become depressed in response to negative events, such as a college student who gets a bad grade.[5] Wayne does not have a depressive attributional style, and so does not have this risk factor.

Inoculated From Catching Depression: A Vaccine for Batman

Believe it or not, emotions can be contagious.[6] When people around you are in a good mood, you're more likely to be, or get into, a good mood. It appears that we tend, unconsciously, to mimic the emotional expressions of others and in doing so induce that mood in ourselves. If someone smiles at you, you're likely to smile (at least more likely to smile than if they frowned at you). If you're around someone who's depressed, you're more likely to become depressed. For example, among college roommates, within three weeks of living with someone who was depressed, the roommate developed symptoms of depression.[7]

Fortunately for Wayne, he doesn't spend a lot of time with people who are depressed. One person he spends a lot of time with is Alfred. Alfred's not the most emotionally demonstrative person on the planet, but after all, he's British. Granted, he doesn't convey a lot of joy, but he doesn't convey a lot of sadness either. He's emotionally rock-steady and uses gentle levity to lighten the mood of the Batcave.

Batman also spends time with Robin, or Robins. The Robins may sometimes be funny and irreverent, irritating or angry, or moody in an adolescent way, but they typically aren't depressed, even when they become adults (e.g., Nightwing, Red Robin). The people closest to Batman thus create a firewall against the emotional contagion of depression.

Relationships

Most often, an episode of depression follows a significantly stressful event: A relationship breakup, the death of a family member or close friend, getting fired, or juggling too many balls at work.[8] (This is particularly true of first episodes of depression.) Like many people who work the front lines of law enforcement or military duty, Wayne experiences such significantly stressful events on a daily, or more accurately, a nightly basis. He repeatedly puts his life at risk as well as the lives of sidekicks who work with him.

If he were going to develop depression at some point, you'd think it would be after the death of someone close to him, such as his parents or Jason Todd, or after the breakup of the handful of intimate relationships he's had with women, such as with Silver St. Cloud or Vicki Vale.* He was sad, yet he didn't get depressed. Why not? One explanation is that the other relationships in his life provide enough support—enough of a buffer—to get him out of the rough patches of the stressful events. Not only does he have Alfred and Dick Grayson, but he's got an extended bat-family. Depending on the specific point in time, the bat-family could include any of the following: Batgirl, Oracle, Jim Gordon, Batwoman, Nightwing, Robin, and Red Robin. Batman also has

---

* In comics, Vicki Vale, a Gotham City reporter, and Bruce had a romantic relationship; during that time, she did not know that Wayne was Batman, though she had suspicions. At the end of the 1989 film *Batman*, Vicki Vale and Wayne begin an intimate relationship in which she knows about his dual identities. In the following film, *Batman Returns*, Wayne mentions that their relationship ended because she wasn't able to handle his dual life.

support, should he make use of it, in his family of superfriends: Superman, Wonder Woman, Green Lantern, Zatanna, Green Arrow, Hawkman and Hawkgirl, Martian Manhunter, Black Canary and so on.

Batman may not always feel warm and fuzzy toward the people in his extended de facto family, but he respects them. He can be himself with them, and they try to support him when they think he needs it. Sure there are conflicts sometimes, just like in any family or group of friends, but his bat-family and super-family live what he lives, and they can relate to his travails and trials. They *know* what he goes through and so their support means something.

Why Might Wayne Get Depressed?

Would I be surprised if Wayne did develop depression? No. Despite the protective factors that work in his favor, he faces a multitude of frustrations and significant stressors on a daily basis and his life entails numerous risk factors associated with depression.

First, the nature of his work shoves in his face the seamy, selfish, even sadistic side of life. Like police officers who confront similar daily horrors, cynicism about life and human nature is a natural outcome. It's hard to feel optimistic or hopeful about the world and the future when you see what Batman sees. And if there's no hope, then what's the point of trying? This question is more than an existential one. It is one that Batman struggles with repeatedly. For instance, the Joker tries to convince Batman of the futility of his actions on many occasions, and crime in Gotham seems to stay the same, or get worse, regardless of Batman's actions. If Batman consistently starts to feel that there isn't any point, then it's very likely he'd slide into depression, as we would if we felt the same way. (In fact, this human superhero might seem more human if he did get depressed.)

Second, if something happened to his support system to leave him isolated, he could get depressed and overwhelmed. Yes, even Batman could get overwhelmed.

Third, Batman could slide into depression if the deaths of other loved ones happened because of his work as the Caped Crusader; their deaths would increase his burden of guilt.

The Take Home Message: Is Batman Depressed?

I don't think Batman is depressed. In fact, I propose that he doesn't have any symptoms of depression. Factors that protect him against depression include his sense of self-efficacy, his attributional style, the fact that those closest to him aren't depressed, and his amply supportive relationships.

His extreme attention to detail, though, might indicate symptoms of a different disorder, as we see in the next chapter.

CHAPTER 4

OBSESSIVE-COMPULSIVE, OR JUST THOROUGH?

Bruce Wayne thinks a lot. Yes, he is a smart guy and some of his thoughts focus on inventing new bat-technologies to help him in his battle against Gotham City's villains. Sometimes we see him sitting in his chair in the Batcave, trying to puzzle out what the Riddler or Two-Face will do next. Other times, we have no idea what he's thinking, nor does Alfred. Perhaps he's obsessing.

Bruce Wayne is also known for being methodical and orderly. Almost "anal." At times his behaviors seem compulsive—that he *has* to do them. Does Wayne have obsessive-compulsive disorder (OCD)? That's the question that I seek to answer in this chapter. At its heart, obsessive-compulsive disorder involves fear—fear about obsessions coming true and fear of not being able to complete the compulsive behaviors. Compulsions usually, but only temporarily, alleviate the fear and anxiety.

Obsessions

According to DSM-IV, *obsessions* are repetitive thoughts or impulses that intrude on someone's awareness and aren't appropriate to the situation or context. These thoughts and impulses typically lead to anxiety. Classic examples are thoughts about whether the stove was turned off or the door locked when leaving home. Someone with OCD gets anxious when such thoughts arise—so anxious that he or she feels compelled to check the stove or the locks *multiple times.*

Obsessions can take a variety of forms. Some people may have intrusive and recurrent thoughts or impulses—such as the impulse to alphabetize the canned goods in the kitchen cupboard. If the person leaves the contents of the cupboard in an unalphabetized state, anxiety ensues. Common obsessions have been sorted into five categories, which involve intrusive thoughts of:

- possible contamination (with dirt or germs);
- disorder or misalignment of household objects;
- hoarding—the urge to save things in the remote case that an object is needed at some undetermined point in the future. An example is someone who doesn't want to throw away the newspaper or empty Amazon boxes because *at some point* these objects could come in handy;
- whether an action was taken, such as turning off the stove (referred to as *doubt*); or,
- possibly losing control—that the person might do something inappropriate or aggressive.

The intrusive nature of these thoughts means that they're hard to turn off. They come unbidden and don't leave very easily. Let's walk through whether Bruce Wayne seems to have any of these common types of obsessions.

Contamination: Don't Touch

Batman certainly doesn't seem preoccupied with germs or dirt, and he is willing to get dirty, both literally and figuratively, to obtain information about Gotham's underworld. He comes into contact with blood, dirt, and whatever else he needs to touch in order to apprehend villains and shut down their nefarious plots.

Disorder (But Not Chaos)

You might make a case that Batman has obsessive thoughts about order because objects in the Batcave have special places. But there's no indication that objects being out of place make Wayne anxious—just concerned, appropriately, that someone's been in the Batcave and moved things around. His desire for order is not obsessive in the sense of a mental illness. Rather, it is a good strategy for a superhero, just as it is for soldiers, officers, firefighters, or anyone else who wants to be able to find a particular object quickly, especially when lives are at stake.

Hoarding: Saving Just Because

What about the urge that some people with OCD have to hoard—to save things "just in case"? Well, Batman does save some objects (such as matches, string, fire retardant foam dispensers and a host of random objects he seems able to pull out that solve any given situation) and the Batcave is full of mementos, at least in the comics. You could make a case that he hoards. I counter that Batman, as a detective and scientist, saves things that actually might be useful to him in the future, rather than true hoarding of objects that are not likely to be useful at a later date. Many of the objects he collects or saves *are* useful—they've saved his life or tripped up a villain (such as a piece of string he happened to have in his utility belt, which helped him escape from a locked cage*). Nonetheless, should Alfred inadvertently throw away something Wayne had saved, it's hard to believe that Wayne would get panicky—which would likely occur if he had OCD.

Doubt: Did I Do That?

Does he seem to doubt whether he performed an action? Generally not, unless he's having memory problems from being knocked unconscious or drugged. Indeed, he couldn't perform his job if he had to return home to check whether he had left on a bat-device.

Loss of Control

Is he preoccupied with losing control? Hmm...at first glance the answer to this question may seem a bit less than clear-cut. When he battles criminals and villains, he must take care to be in control, especially when he's riled up or angry. If he loses control he could use more force than needed, otherwise he could unnecessarily injure or kill. After all, Jim Gordon and the folks in Gotham City's correctional and judicial systems

---

* This happened in *Batman #37* (1946).

allow him to be a "vigilante" as long as he remains on the right side of the law and uses no more force than necessary. Although he may be preoccupied with being in control, it's for a good reason. It's appropriate to the situation—unlike true obsessions, which are not appropriate to the situation.

Compulsions

Perhaps Wayne has an uncommon obsession that isn't captured by the list of five common types. If so, odds are that he'd have some corresponding compulsion as well. In fact, people with obsessive-compulsive disorder usually have compulsions along with obsessions. *Compulsions* are repetitive behaviors (such as going back to check that the door is locked) or mental acts (such as counting to 10) that the person feels driven—compelled—to perform.

Compulsions can feel almost ritualistic, and if the person doesn't complete the behavior or mental act, he or she may get quite anxious or agitated. Compulsions are either: not realistically connected to the worries or fears that drive them *or* they are *extreme* attempts to address the underlying concerns. The compulsions must be behaviors or mental acts that the person feels internally forced to do—over and over again—in order to reduce or prevent anxiety, distress, or some "bad" event. The compulsions, however, aren't realistically related to the anxiety, distress, or untoward event and are excessive. So excessive that people with OCD may not be able to leave the house because their compulsions take many hours.

As part of the criteria for OCD, the person, at some point, is aware that the obsessions and/or compulsions are excessive. Moreover, the mental or physical activities must take more than one hour each day or otherwise interfere with the person's work, family life, social life, or other normal daily activities.

Does Bruce Wayne have any compulsions? We don't know much about his physical training regimen, so we can't say whether that's a compulsion. In fact, we rarely see him spending the hours he must put in to maintain his amazing physique, quick reflexes, and physical endurance. But we know that he has to spend hours each day exercising.[*]

If you were to make a case that Wayne has compulsions, you might point to the endless hours he spends thinking about criminals and how to apprehend

---

[*] For information about the effort it would actually take to have Batman's physique, strength, and stamina, I suggest you read Paul Zehr's book *Becoming Batman*.

them. About getting into their mindset. About preparing to take them on. Even when he's going about Bruce Wayne's business, he's often thinking about Batman's business—about weapons he can devise or use, or ways to foil possible criminal plans. Painted in this light, such planning could be construed as compulsive mental acts. However, to be considered true compulsions, these mental acts must be either excessive or not realistically connected to the events they are trying to prevent. He doesn't count to 100 after having a troublesome thought or after behaving in a way that makes him uncomfortable.

Whatever mental acts or compulsive-seeming behaviors he engages in, they *are* realistically connected to his trying to preempt villains' plans, to apprehend them, or to save Gotham's citizens in some way. Trying to figure out where the Riddler might next strike is an appropriate thought for Bruce Wayne, particularly if the Riddler isn't locked safely away in Arkham Asylum or Blackgate Prison. (As if being in either of those places has held off the villains from plotting further escapades!)

As Bruce Wayne notes about his dedication to crimefighting:

> People think it's an obsession. A compulsion. As if there were an irresistible impulse to act. It's never

been like that. I chose this life. I know what I'm doing. And on any given day, I could stop doing it. Today, however, isn't that day. And tomorrow won't be either.*

Thus, the diagnosis of OCD isn't appropriate, at least in its typical presentation.

An Atypical Case of OCD?

I've laid out my reasoning about why he doesn't have the typical kinds of obsessions. But he does spend a lot of time thinking about Gotham City's criminals. A case could be made that the thoughts are intrusive, because he has a hard time turning them off. These thoughts crowd out other things in his life. Moreover, the time, mental energy, and physical energy he spends as Batman (whether in costume or not) seem to be a compulsion. Although he may think he has a choice (as noted in the quote above) at times it seems as if he can't help himself but to be the Batman.

But the same could be said about anyone's passionate interests. People fortunate enough to have a job or hobby to which they are dedicated will have intrusive thoughts about it and will put in more time

---

* In Brad Meltzer's story, *Identity Crisis* (2004).

than necessary. (In fact, isn't that what hobbies are? In a sense, Wayne's pursuit of criminals is a deadly serious full-time hobby from which Gotham's citizens benefit.) People who are passionate about their work willingly put in many more hours than required for the job—and will think about it even when they're not physically at work. Similarly, people newly in love or "in like" will have intrusive thoughts about the new partner, and may find themselves feeling compelled to send emails or text messages to the partner, or to buy presents or perform other acts.[9]

Wayne doesn't appear to have an atypical case of OCD; whatever preoccupying thoughts and compulsive-like behaviors he has, they don't seem to cause him distress, they certainly don't impair his ability to function, and the preoccupying thoughts and compulsive-like behaviors don't increase his risk of harm. In fact, given that he's going to fight Gotham's criminals, his thorough planning and methodical preparation decrease his risk of harm to himself: He is as prepared as anyone can be.

Obsessive-Compulsive Personality Disorder?

A related disorder in DSM-IV is *obsessive-compulsive personality disorder*. DSM-IV contains ten personality disorders, each of which specifies that at least some of the specific symptoms must have arisen during childhood. Because the symptoms began during childhood, the theory goes, the symptoms become an integral part of the person's identity. Moreover, someone with a personality disorder typically doesn't think he or she has a problem. Rather, the person with a personality disorder thinks that the problem is with other people or with situations.

Obsessive-compulsive personality disorder focuses on traits that emphasize rigidly striving for orderliness, perfection, and control of self and others, causing decreased flexibility and spontaneity—rather than specific obsessions and compulsions. To be diagnosed with this personality disorder, an individual must have at least four of the eight symptoms described below, and the symptoms must have begun in childhood.

Preoccupation With Rules, Order, Organization

People with obsessive-compulsive personality disorder are so preoccupied with organizing details (e.g., making lists or schedules) that they lose the point of the activity. For instance, when writing a paper or preparing for a talk, people with this symptom spend an inordinate amount of time organizing the material. Batman might organize the schedule of events for a complicated plan to apprehend Poison Ivy, but he never loses the big picture.

Extreme Perfectionism: Got To Do It Right

Folks with this symptom are so bent on getting a task as perfect as possible (e.g., "getting it right") that they have a hard time finishing the task. This symptom might apply to Batman if he were to miss opportunities to intervene with criminals because he was spending too much time perfecting his plan. But this doesn't happen, so Batman doesn't have this symptom.

Workaholism: So Much To Do, So Little Time

This symptom focuses on extreme devotion to work, to the point where friendships and "down time" are sacrificed. People with this symptom typically get agitated on vacations if they're not getting some work done while away from work. (If someone's extreme focus on work is because of financial need—working double shifts to pay the bills—that behavior wouldn't be considered a symptom of obsessive-compulsive personality disorder.)

This symptom clearly applies to Wayne. He rarely, if ever, lets himself have down time or vacations, most of his friends are colleagues, and his most important romantic relationships typically end, in essence, because of his devotion to his work. Moreover, he undoubtedly exhibited this symptom before adulthood; it was soon after his parents' deaths that he made the decision to avenge his their deaths. Though we don't know much about his childhood and teen years, we can reasonably infer that his intense physical, mental, or intellectual training began before adulthood.

Overconscientious Morality

The fourth symptom of obsessive-compulsive personality disorder is inflexible values, morality, or ethics, and being scrupulous about applying these values, morals or ethics (either to themselves or others). So scrupulous that it becomes a problem in some aspect of daily life.

A case could be made that Batman's morality and values are inflexible (e.g., don't kill—even the Joker) and that he applies these standards inflexibly to himself. I don't think so, though. His principle about not taking a life is shared by many people (including those opposed to the death penalty), and his fervent adherence to this principle does not seem overly scrupulous to me. It is this line that he feels separates him from the villains he tries to apprehend. Perhaps the best example of this occurred when the Justice League of America decided to wipe the mind of the villain Doctor Light so that he wouldn't continue to harm the friends and family of Justice League members. Batman alone refused to accept this decision, and the League members decided to wipe Batman's own memory of the encounter—against his will.

Hoarding

The one symptom of obsessive-compulsive personality disorder that directly corresponds to OCD is that of hoarding—keeping things that are worthless or too worn, even when the object doesn't have any sentimental value (such as last month's newspaper). As noted earlier in this chapter, Wayne doesn't have this symptom.

Miser: Don't Spend!

People with this symptom are misers, hoarding their money in case of a future catastrophe. This definitely is not the case with Batman.

Doesn't Delegate

Someone with the sixth symptom of obsessive-compulsive personality disorder has a hard time delegating tasks to others—unless the tasks are done exactly as he or she wants them done. Batman is very exacting in how he wants things done—how villains are approached, how their plans are foiled. He trains his Robins hard, and won't let them out in the field until he determines that they're ready, which means that they'd do things as *he* wants them to do it. If he's going to *have* young sidekicks, though, he's wise to be so exacting with them, to make sure they do what he says, when he says. Their lives are at stake.

In other realms of his life, he has no problems delegating responsibility and the execution of tasks for Wayne Foundation or Wayne Enterprises, and he delegates to Alfred many other tasks of his life as Bruce Wayne. His difficulty delegating is limited to dangerous tasks related to stopping criminals; I think that is (mostly) appropriate. He doesn't want to be responsible if other people get hurt because he asked them to do something for him. (It perplexes me how he takes in sidekicks on the one hand, yet has difficulty asking for help from the adults in his life, such as Alfred or Batgirl, on the other hand. This is one of his many paradoxes.)

Rigid and Stubborn

People with this symptom of obsessive-compulsive personality disorder are more than simply stubborn; they are so stubborn and rigid in their behaviors and thinking that it creates problems at work or in their relationships. Batman may be a somewhat controlling workaholic and think his way is the right way (and it often is), but he's not rigid. When someone else's suggestion is right, he acknowledges it, such as when Superman brings up a more efficient way of solving a problem or when Robin suggests an alternate method of attack. This was not a trait the Silver St. Cloud or other women in his life mention when the talk about the difficulties of being Bruce Wayne's/Batman's girlfriend.

The Take Home Message: Is Batman Truly Obsessive or Compulsive?

In my opinion, Wayne has neither OCD nor obsessive-compulsive personality disorder. He doesn't have intrusive obsessions, nor does he have compulsions—behaviors that he feels *driven* to do in order to minimize anxiety. He does seem to have some personality traits related to obsessive-compulsive personality disorder, such as being a workaholic and having an over-conscientious morality, but these traits don't reach the level necessary for a diagnosis of that personality disorder.

However, as I discuss in the next chapter, he definitely meets at least one criterion for the diagnosis of posttraumatic stress disorder: He's experienced a traumatic event. In fact, he's experienced many.

CHAPTER 5

POSTTRAUMATIC STRESS DISORDER?

As a child, long before Wayne became the Batman, he'd experienced a significant traumatic event: he witnessed the senseless murder of his parents by a thug, and his own life was in danger as well. This event cast a long and profound shadow over the rest of his life. Did Wayne end up developing posttraumatic stress disorder (PTSD) as a result?

PTSD: The Criteria

According to DSM-IV, there are five basic criteria

for the diagnosis of PTSD. In order to be diagnosed with the disorder, the individual—in this case, Bruce Wayne—must have symptoms that meet *all* five criteria, below.

Exposed to a Traumatic Event

In order to be diagnosed with PTSD, the person must have been exposed to a traumatic event at which:

- The person saw, experienced, or otherwise encountered a situation that involved the threat of—or actual—serious injury or death to self or another person. This was clearly true of young Bruce Wayne. And,

- The person then responded with horror, fear, or helplessness.

Bruce appeared to have all three responses. The various stories that contain versions of this origin story clearly show young Bruce's expressions of fear and helplessness. For instance, immediately after his mother is shot, "The boy's eyes are wide with terror and shock as the horrible scene is spread before him" (*Batman* #1).

In fact, in inventing the character of Batman, his creators Bob Kane and Bill Finger reportedly declared that, "there's nothing more traumatic than having your parents murdered before your eyes."

Persistently Re-experiences the Traumatic Situation

Memories, flashbacks, dreams, or nightmares are all ways that a traumatic situation can be re-experienced. For this criterion, however, these re-experiences must be persistent, distressing, and intrusive.

In various stories, Wayne has memories, dreams, nightmares, or flashbacks of his parents' deaths.[*] However, these experiences aren't persistent, and the memories don't usually come to him unbidden (except in dreams), they aren't generally intrusive, and he usually retrieves the memories in a normal way.

Persistently Avoids Trauma-Related Stimuli, and Is Numb

This criterion has two difference facets: *avoidance* and *emotional numbing*. Symptoms of avoidance involve attempts to avoid stimuli, memories, or thoughts related to the traumatic event. Avoidance does not seem to apply to Wayne. In the 1989 Tim Burton *Batman* film, for instance, Wayne visits the alley where the murder took place at least annually, and in none of the other versions of Batman that I've read or seen does he generally shy

---

[*] In film, an example is in *Batman Forever* (1995), and in comic books, an example is in *Batman: Blind Justice* (1989).

away from many of the other trauma-related cues: dark streets, being at the wrong end of the barrel of a gun, or encountering menacing people who intend to carry out nefarious deeds. He even goes out of his way to get himself into such situations.

The other facet of this general criterion is emotional numbness, which is indicated by:

- a sense of being detached from others;
- not experiencing very strong positive feelings such as love or joy;
- a sense of shortened mortality, indicated by not expecting to live a long time or to have a family; or,
- significantly less interest or participation in regular activities.

Wayne has significant and deep relationships with Dick Grayson and other young people who assume the role of Robin, as well as Alfred Pennyworth, Superman, and Police Commissioner James Gordon (whom Wayne referred to as one of his oldest friends[*]). Moreover, he has had serious relationships with various women who have more than intrigued him, such as Julie Madison (Wayne's first serious girlfriend), Silver St. Cloud (a later serious girlfriend), Selina Kyle

---

[*] In *Batman Special #1* (1984).

(Catwoman), Talia Head (a.k.a. as Talia al Ghul; she is the daughter of Ra's al Ghul), and Vicki Vale.

One could argue that although Wayne has relationships, he's detached in all of them—even the closest ones, in which case the first symptom of emotional numbing would apply to him. The second symptom of emotional numbing—a lack of strong positive feelings—could also seem to apply: it's rare to see Wayne with a full smile or genuine laugh, let alone a sense of joy or happiness. It's not clear whether Wayne has a sense of shortened mortality, but he clearly wants to live as long as he can to fight against crime and injustice, so this symptom of emotional numbing doesn't seem to apply.

How about the last symptom of emotional numbing—less interest or participation in regular activities? This symptom is meant to indicate that the person has diminished interest in activities directly because of the traumatic event; that is, he or she has lost interest in things previously enjoyed. In dedicating his life to fighting crime, Wayne gave up the "normal" pursuits that he might have followed. His single-minded devotion to crime fighting comes at the cost of partaking in regular activities—an *indirect* result of the traumatic event. (In contrast, a *direct* result would be indicated by flashbacks or lack of normal interest in activities because of feeling "nothing.")

In sum, it seems that Wayne may have at least the first two symptoms of emotional numbing (detachment and muted positive emotions), but probably not the last two.

Persistently Increased Arousal

Increased arousal is indicated by sleep problems, concentration problems, angry outbursts and increased irritability, being easily startled, and being hypervigilant for "danger." In order to meet this general arousal criterion, the symptoms must not have been characteristic of the person before the trauma, but rather emerged after it.

Batman—a mere human—is considered a superhero because of his phenomenal physical and mental abilities. Despite being somewhat prone to brooding, he is generally even-tempered. He is able to focus on the task at hand, use flawless logic and planning, and channel his emotions so that they help him to accomplish his goals. He generally doesn't panic, have outbursts, or appear to be irritable. When angry, he does on occasion use more force than necessary, beating criminals well after they've given up, as he does in

Batman: Strange Apparitions,[*] after Silver St. Cloud breaks off their relationship.

In fact, the only aspect of increased arousal that Wayne seems to have is a hypervigilance for danger. Like a police officer walking a beat, or a detective taking part in an undercover operation, Batman has his antennae up for possible danger, but hypervigilance is normal in that context. Batman is always on duty, and so it makes sense that he would be preternaturally attuned for possible threats.

Clinically Significant Distress or Impairment

Even if Batman had symptoms that met all four of the previous criteria, would he be diagnosed with PTSD? Not necessarily. Once the person is found to have met all of the above criteria for at least a month, according to DSM-IV, he or she is still only diagnosed with PTSD if the symptoms cause "clinically significant distress, or impairment in social, occupational, or other important areas of functioning."[10]

As a wealthy person without a 9-to-5 job that requires a moderately high level of functioning, he has a lot more flexibility than your average Joe or Jane. Given

---

[*] In the 1999 collection, based on *Detective Comics* #469-476, 478, 479 (1977-1978).

the fact that he is a billionaire whose time is his own, in what ways could it be said that his functioning is impaired?

Clearly his work life isn't impaired. He seems to carry out his duties with Wayne Enterprises and Wayne Foundation effectively. Is he impaired because his life is narrowed by his devotion to fighting crime? If so, then the same could be said of heart surgeons, firefighters, police officers, and counterintelligence operatives who devote their lives (literally, in some cases) to the same ultimate cause—saving the lives of others.

Moreover, Wayne's social life is no more impaired than that of many other extremely wealthy people, and if we compare him to other ridiculously rich people (think Paris Hilton), he looks downright emotionally stable. He has close friendships and can have intimate relationships with women—at least as intimate as is possible given the secret he guards. So while he doesn't have a normal life, I don't think his functioning is significantly impaired.

Does He Have PTSD?

Wayne definitely suffered a traumatic event, but does he have enough symptoms of PTSD to merit the diagnosis? The only symptoms he has are those related to emotional numbing, and these may be a by-product of the emotional deadening necessary to dedicate his life to fighting crime as the Caped Crusader. Thus, his behavior and experiences don't meet enough of the criteria for him to be diagnosed with PTSD. Wayne may be weird in some ways, but it's not because he has PTSD.

Why He Doesn't Have PTSD: Resilient Master Wayne

Witnessing the murder of one's parents is clearly traumatic, and you may be surprised that Batman doesn't have PTSD, given this experience. However, not everyone who has experienced a trauma goes on to develop PTSD. In fact, most traumatized people *don't* develop this disorder.[11] Most people emerge from a traumatic event without PTSD because the traumatic event they experienced was a one-time situation. Moreover, traumatic events that are less personal (such as those incurred as a result of a natural disaster) are less likely to lead to PTSD than are traumatic events that are personal (such as rape[12]).

People who don't develop PTSD after a trauma also are likely to have possessed *protective factors*—factors that are associated with resiliency in the face of a trauma. One such factor is intelligence, which is thought to provide people with more options for coping with the traumatic event.[13] Wayne certainly has a high IQ.

Another protective factor relates to the way people cope after the trauma. Wayne coped the way many other trauma survivors do: by making meaning of the traumatic event. The risk of PTSD decreases if the traumatized person can understand the trauma in a larger framework about the meaning of life.[14] Such meaning has three aspects:[15]

- *Global beliefs*—beliefs related to the idea that there is justice and fairness in the world.[16] Before experiencing a significant trauma, most people believe that the world is a reasonably fair place and that they can control important aspects of their lives;

- *Global goals*—what people strive for: achievements, work, knowledge, or relationships.

- *Subjective feelings of meaning*—feeling that life has a purpose. This is often related to the individual's global goals.[17] Prior to experiencing a traumatic event, most people feel that they're achieving their global goals.[18]

Traumatic events can call into question people's global beliefs, and cause them to question their global goals.[19] The purpose of life becomes unclear as people come to terms in a deep way with the fact that life isn't always fair, that bad things can happen to good people, and we can't always control what happens to us and our loved ones. To come to terms with trauma, people must make new meaning out of life. They must rethink their beliefs and question their goals. As their beliefs and goals come into new alignment, they often feel a new sense of purpose—the trauma has induced them to grow.[20]

This growth process was true for Wayne. In dedicating his life to fighting crime, he gave his life new meaning: new beliefs (about justice and fairness), new goals (obtaining the skills needed to fight crime), and a new purpose (protecting innocent lives and apprehending criminals). And like many trauma survivors, Wayne's version of making meaning involves social activism. Wayne's specific form of social activism is two-fold: First, through the efforts of his charitable organization (which seeks to prevent people from choosing a life of crime and help those who become its victims), and second, by putting his life on the line each night:

> I heard the cries of the dying . . . and the mourning . . . the victims of crime and injustice . . . I swore I'd do everything in my

power to avenge those deaths . . . to protect innocent lives.[*]

The way that Wayne has made meaning out of his traumatic experience lends itself to seriousness; lives are continually at stake. All of the weird aspects of Wayne's life—being a loner, brooding, having dual identities, and seeking danger while dressed up in a costume—arise from his chosen path of social activism. Seen through the lens of meaning-making, many of Wayne's quirks of behavior lose their weirdness. They seem to be the consequence of an incredibly bright, talented, and altruistic young man's decision to give up the semblance of a normal life for a greater good.

The Take Home Message: Does Batman Have PTSD?

Wayne didn't develop PTSD as a result of this first trauma. However, as Batman he experiences or witnesses significant violence and risks his life on a weekly if not nightly basis. He even has had his back broken by the villain Bane.[†] You'd think that these events would lead to PTSD. (And if they don't, maybe his

---

[*] *Batman and the Outsiders* #1 (1983).

[†] In *Batman #497* (1993), part of the *Knightfall* storyline written by Doeg Moench.

superpower is that he's invulnerable to PTSD?) Yet he doesn't develop PTSD as an adult for the same reasons that he didn't develop PTSD as a result of his childhood trauma. He has enough protective factors—his wealth, his intelligence, his dedication to his mission, support from his friends and surrogate family—that he is able to view the traumas he incurs nightly as part of the job. He expects his evenings to be filled with people attacking him. He isn't disappointed.

But his career choice raises some eyebrows about whether being a vigilante is an indication of a disorder. That's the topic of the next chapter.

CHAPTER 6

ANTISOCIAL PERSONALITY

DISORDER?

Some people refer to Batman as a vigilante. In fact, various of his actions skirt the law if not break it, and when he does break the law, he doesn't seem to feel guilty or remorseful. These qualities are elements of two psychological problems: psychopathy and antisocial personality disorder, which are the focus of this chapter.

Psychopathy

Psychopathy is the name given to the set of

personality traits and behaviors of people who seem to break or skirt the law chronically, take advantage of others, and leave others' lives scarred. People with psychopathy are called psychopaths. Some psychopaths are in jail or locked in mental institutions (such as the Joker); other psychopaths are in boardrooms and offices. Psychopathy involves problems with four clusters of symptoms: relationships, emotions, lifestyle, and behaviors.[21] By the way, psychopathy is not a "diagnosis." It's not in DSM-IV, and it's not considered a mental disorder or mental illness. Rather, the term refers to a set of specific personality traits and behaviors.

Relationships: Problems From Inflated Self-Worth and Tendency to Lie

One group of problems of psychopathy is with relationships, and such problems arise from an overly inflated sense of self-worth and a tendency to lie or manipulate people, often by being charming—at least initially. Is Bruce Wayne's sense of worth too high? To my mind, no. He's wealthy, handsome, and incredibly capable in so many domains. However well he thinks of himself, he seems to have earned a high self-worth by ability and effort.

I concede that Batman does lie. But not in the

way that psychopaths lie—simply for the fun of pulling one over on people, or to con them for personal gain. When Bruce Wayne lies, he is trying to protect his identity, protect other people, or apprehend or ensnare criminals.

Emotions: Little Empathy or Remorse

Another group of problems involves emotions, specifically a lack of remorse or guilt about harming other people or of violating their rights. Psychopaths also have little or no empathy for other people's plights. In addition, psychopaths appear to have primarily superficial emotions (sometimes referred to as *proto-emotions*); their emotional displays are like those of actors who "put on" emotions that may appear convincing initially.

Typically, psychopaths blame other people for their problems. Batman may show little emotion, but he certainly has empathy for the plights of others—at least for people who aren't criminals. It's one of the reasons that he dons the cape and cowl and goes on his nightly prowls. Batman also shows, at times, touching concern for the safety and well-being of the Robins (although he usually conveys it in a rather abrasive way). I'll discuss in detail the question of whether he feels guilty for harming others later, but for now let's say that generally he tries to avoiding harming innocent people—in contrast to psychopaths who search for innocent people to con.

Lifestyle: Feeding Off of Others Like a Vampire

Psychopaths have lifestyle problems—they are predatory. Psychopaths are generally irresponsible, impulsive, mooch off of others, don't have realistic long-term goals, and get bored easily. They crave stimulation. Wayne may have problems with his lifestyle, but not like those of a psychopath. Whereas Wayne's lifestyle issues arise from his decision to be the Batman and the personal sacrifices that entails, psychopaths often have problems holding jobs, staying in relationships and staying out of trouble not only because they seek "excitement" but because they are impulsive, callous, and lie. The Joker is a psychopath.*

Behavior: Antisocial Behaviors

People with psychopathy engage in behaviors that are problematic from either a legal or antisocial

---

* In most versions of the Joker, his qualities lead to the conclusion that he is a psychopath: He lies and manipulates people, shows no remorse for the harm he causes others, he's predatory, and engages in antisocial behavior.

perspective, indicated by a childhood history of juvenile delinquency as well as a history of recklessness as an adult. Perhaps Wayne was antisocial in his youth? We don't know much about Bruce Wayne's high school years, but it seems certain that he wasn't arrested for delinquent behavior. Any *apparent* reckless behavior in his adult life, I propose, is usually calculated or is not nearly as reckless as it appears because of his rigorous training.

The Take Home Message: Is He a Psychopath?

People can be taken in by psychopaths because they're initially charming and funny, but after a while, most people realize that they're being taken in or taken advantage of. They're being conned—to hand over their life savings for some investment, to loan their car (which is never returned), to provide the extra set of keys to their apartment or house. That's not who Bruce Wayne is—in the cowl or out of it. No psychopath is he.

Antisocial Personality Disorder

The DSM-IV does include a psychiatric disorder related to the behaviors of psychopathy; it's called *antisocial personality disorder*. Antisocial personality disorder is a different type of disorder than most of the ones discussed in other chapters; like obsessive-compulsive personality disorder, it is a *personality disorder*, with symptoms beginning before adulthood. With antisocial personality disorder, the symptoms must have been present since at least age 15.

Compared to psychopathy—which focuses on emotions, motives, relationships, and antisocial behaviors—antisocial personality disorder focuses more narrowly on behaviors, and a narrower range of behaviors at that. The hallmark of this personality disorder is a longstanding trail of behaviors that indicate a disregard for the rights and feelings of others. Below are the symptoms of antisocial personality disorder.

Illegal Acts

People with antisocial personality disorder repeatedly engage in illegal acts that could lead to arrest. Does this symptom apply to Batman? Yes. Even though he's informally deputized by the police department (in most stories), he is not a legitimate arm of the law. He is usually considered a vigilante (or almost one) and he could be arrested for some of his actions as Batman. The illegality and vigilante aspects of his behavior come up in various storylines.

Lie or Con

Another symptom is repeatedly lying, which includes providing false identities or "conning" others for financial advantage or pleasure. Bruce Wayne certainly lies, gives false identities and sometimes cons others, but it isn't for financial advantage. Is it for pleasure? Not in the sense intended for this diagnosis, and even if Batman did get pleasure from lying to Two-Face or other villains, Batman's primary motivation isn't pleasure. Any pleasure he experiences from his lying or conning is because it leads him to foil villains' plans. He does *not* get pleasure from lying to the women in his life when he hides the aspects of his life as Batman. This symptom doesn't apply to him.

Impulsive

People with antisocial personality disorder often are impulsive or chronically fail to plan ahead. Not true of Batman. He rarely acts impulsively and one of his hallmarks is his ability to think of multiple fall-back options and to plan for almost any eventuality.

Fight

Folks with antisocial personality disorder tend to get into physical fights or to assault others, and these actions are presumed (according to the DSM-IV) to be motivated by the person's irritability or aggression. Batman certainly does fight and assault others (and sometimes he feels particularly aggressive while doing so). But he does so in order to deter or apprehend criminals. He's not generally motivated by aggression for its own sake. As Bruce Wayne he is very rarely irritable, let alone aggressive, unless it is a strategic act. Exceptions when Batman has seemed motivated by aggression have usually involved the Joker: punching Superman after Jason Todd's death and his general attitude toward other people after the Joker shot Barbara Gordon.

Given the number of villains and criminals that Batman has encountered, it's remarkable how few people he has significantly hurt.* In contrast, the fights of people with antisocial personality disorder are rarely in the service of a larger goal or greater good, and tend to be impulsive.

Reckless

Another symptom of this personality disorder is a pattern of neglecting one's own safety or that of other people; this recklessness is assumed to be a by-product

---

* Even after DC Comics stopped using the comics code authority guidelines.

of the pursuit of profit or pleasure. Is Batman reckless? Part of being a crime fighter is—at some level— neglecting one's own safety. But Batman takes calculated risks, and makes sure that he's as well-prepared as possible when he may have to go into battle.

That said, our Caped Crusader is more reckless when it comes to the safety of others. As I discussed in Chapter 1, he puts at risk the lives of various Robins who have been his sidekicks over the years by allowing them to join his fight against crime in an active, physically-endangering way. Yet Batman doesn't simply let the youngsters run wild. He trains them intensively, and won't give them the go-ahead to don the little yellow cape until he determines that they're ready.[*] Even after they wear the cape, he'll ground Robin when he feels that he (or she) isn't in control enough to fight safely.[†]

Nonetheless, he does endanger the lives of others, and this is certainly true of some of the innocent Gotham City lives he is trying to protect: in Batman's pursuit of the villains, he endangers the lives of bystanders. In the

---

[*] As happened with Jason Todd, Tim Drake, Stephanie Brown, and Damian Wayne.

[†] As Wayne did with Jason Todd, which led Todd to go off on his own to find his mother (*A Death in the Family* story), and with Damian Wayne after his son punched Tim Drake (*Batman and Son* story).

chase scenes in any of the Christopher Nolan *Batman* films, for instance, drivers who happen to be near Batman's path while he's pursuing his prey are in danger as cars collide and turn over. More directly, Batman's presence at most crime scenes increases the danger to everyone present: Criminals become more likely to grab hostages and seem to become trigger-happy as soon as they see the Caped Crusader.

To the extent that Batman is reckless, though, it's not in pursuit of profit or pleasure—it's to apprehend dangerous criminals. At this point, I say he doesn't have this symptom of antisocial personality disorder.

Shirk Responsibility

Antisocial personality disorder is often characterized by a pattern of shirking work and financial responsibilities, based on an underlying general tendency toward irresponsibility. This symptom definitely does not apply to Batman although sometimes his duties as Batman may cause him to delay fulfilling some of his duties with Wayne Enterprises or the Wayne Foundation. For example, he might arrive late to a charitable function because he was working as Batman.

However, if Wayne were not wealthy and so had to hold down a regular job, he might well have to choose between shirking his job as Batman in order to work for a paycheck or shirking his day job and his paycheck in order to work as Batman. This is a dilemma that Peter Parker (Spider-Man) and other non-wealthy superheroes must face. Thankfully for Gotham City, Wayne is wealthy and doesn't have to choose.

No Guilt, No Regrets

Like psychopaths, people with antisocial personality disorder exhibit a fundamental lack of genuine guilt or regret for hurting or stealing from others, and rationalize why such actions are acceptable or reasonable. Is Batman indifferent to the effects his actions have on others?

With villains, Batman generally contains himself and doesn't inflict more harm than necessary to capture or restrain his foes. Occasionally, however, Batman crosses the line, experiences regret at his lack of control, and he uses it as an opportunity to learn how to control himself more effectively. In contrast, Batman seems unaware of the harm to ordinary citizens that he inadvertently causes in his battles with villains. He doesn't seem to regret it because he doesn't register it. Consider this quote from the film *Batman Begins*:

Alfred Pennyworth: When you told me your grand

plan for saving Gotham, the only thing that stopped me from calling the men in white coats was when you said that it wasn't about thrill-seeking.

Bruce Wayne: It's not.

Alfred Pennyworth: What would you call *that*?

> [*points to a TV news report showing a helicopter shot of the Batmobile being chased down the freeway by police cars*]

Bruce Wayne: [*as he fixes his tie*] Damn good television.

Alfred Pennyworth: It's a miracle no one was killed.

Bruce Wayne: Didn't have time to observe the rules of the road, Alfred.

Unlike most people with antisocial personality disorder, though, Batman doesn't set out to inflict harm on innocents. To the contrary, ultimately he's trying to protect them.* In his pursuit of villains, though, innocents do get hurt and Batman does not appear to experience significant or deep regret about it. Furthermore, incredibly expensive damage is inflicted on property as Batman tries to apprehend villains; as far as the stories reveal, Wayne does not underwrite the costs

---

* For instance, in *Batman: Arkham City* by Paul Dini and Carlos D'Anda (2011), before going into a dangerous situation in Arkham City, Batman explains to Catwoman that he doesn't want to call in other members of his "bat-pack" because he doesn't want them to get hurt. He, however, is willing to get hurt.

of rebuilding.

The Take Home Message: Does Batman Have Antisocial Personality Disorder?

Wayne may disregard the rights and feelings of criminals, but he doesn't generally and actively disregard the rights and feelings of noncriminals. By my analysis, Wayne seems to have at most two of the symptoms of antisocial personality disorder: Illegal acts and no guilt. For a diagnosis of antisocial personality disorder, though, he'd need to have three or more. Plus the symptoms have to have been present since at least age 15; I haven't come across any stories that indicate the high-school age Bruce Wayne exhibited these symptoms. Rather, they most likely manifested themselves after he was an adult, around the time when The Batman came into existence.

CHAPTER 7

IS ANYTHING THE MATTER WITH BATMAN?

At first blush, it's easy to think that there must be something psychologically wrong with Bruce Wayne, with Batman. He's a really odd billionaire in so many ways. He dresses up as a giant bat to fight crime and lives a secret and dangerous life. In doing so he's created dual identities for himself. He shares all these aspects with covert operatives and undercover police officers, and shares dual identities and a secret life with homosexuals in the closet and other people hiding an aspect of their lives. But as I explained in Chapter 2, this doesn't mean he has dissociative identity disorder.

In addition, Batman is neither chatty nor of sunny disposition; he may not be "happy," but that doesn't necessarily mean he's depressed. As I noted in Chapter 3, I *don't* think that he's depressed. I think he's a serious man, made so certainly by events in his life but perhaps also by temperament.

As I explained in Chapter 4, just because he's a meticulous planner, thorough and puts things in their place, that doesn't mean he has obsessive-compulsive disorder. He doesn't. Nor does he have obsessive-compulsive personality disorder (though he has elements of it).

As discussed, Batman has had more than his share of traumas in his life. Yet, remarkably, he does not appear to have enough symptoms to meet the criteria for posttraumatic stress disorder (Chapter 5). He's shown incredible resilience in the face of his past and current traumas. And although he might see himself as somewhat outside or above the law as he deals with Gotham's criminal element, he doesn't have antisocial personality disorder, nor is a psychopath, as I explained in Chapter 6.

These disorders are the ones Wayne would be most likely to have based on the odd or problematic characteristics he exhibits. But he doesn't have these disorders (or others). Is this all that could be wrong with Batman, a tendency to be obsessive and compulsive?

People can be odd, be weird, be quirky, but not necessarily have a psychiatric disorder. They can be different than "normal" but not be abnormal. This, I think, is part of the lesson that Batman teaches us. Batman is an amazing human superhero, and Bruce Wayne is an amazing, albeit fictional, human being. He found a silver lining in the dark cloud of witnessing the murders of his parents: to apprehend criminals and protect innocents. This is an admirable and worthy mission, and such a selfless pursuit in-and-of-itself does not indicate that there is anything "the matter" with him. In fact, its worthiness helps insulate him from developing psychological problems associated with disorders. His belief that he is ultimately doing good, reinforced by hearing things like a little boy say "Batman will save us" in *Batman Begins*, protects him psychologically.

His beliefs allow him to put in a larger context the sadism he witnesses and the violence in which he participates. Moreover, unlike most people who are victims of violent crime, Batman doesn't see himself as a victim in his situations with villains; this view helps him to feel in control in dangerous situations and less likely to develop psychological problems. Indeed, his sense of agency and control is likely what inoculated him from paralyzing depression.

The worthiness of his mission isn't the only thing that helps insulate Batman from developing a psychiatric disorder as he fights Gotham's criminals and villains. Batman has a strong support team. Granted, he may not make as much use of it as he could or as his friends would like. But his support team knows how to support him. Alfred knows when to step in and when to step back, as do Dick Grayson and other adult members of the bat-family. His superfriends in the Justice League accept and support him, foibles and all.[*]

---

[*] His superfriends are not always so supportive, such as when the Justice League decided that Batman's mind should be wiped after the incident with Doctor Light (discussed in Chapter 5). Here's what happened in the comic storyline *Identity Crisis* in 2004: The Justice League (without Batman present) voted for fellow member and magician Zatana to use her powers to transform the personality of villainous Dr. Light so that he would not continue to attack family members of superheroes. (He had previously brutally raped and killed Elongated Man's wife, Sue Dibny, and threatened to do similar deeds to other Justice League family members.) Batman came upon the scene and didn't agree with the League members' decision; the rest of the Justice League voted to erase Batman's memory of the incident with Dr. Light. Batman later discovered that this memory had been erased and he viewed it, understandably, as a betrayal. They had to earn his trust anew.

However, let's be clear: Most people don't dress up and become vigilantes who wear capes and cowls. Just because Wayne doesn't have a diagnosable psychiatric disorder (in my opinion) doesn't mean that he doesn't have issues. That's part of what's behind the question "what's the matter with Batman?" You might point to his relationships with women. I counter that they may be less than ideal, but he's capable of being in an intimate relationship with a woman, and he's had several very meaningful relationships, with Rachel Dawes (in *Batman Begins*), Silver St. Cloud, and even Catwoman. Moreover, Bruce Wayne is not alone in his lack of success in making a relationship work over the long haul. Most people's intimate relationships don't work out. (If you want "proof" of this, aside for the almost 50% divorce rate, consider how many relationships you and your friends have had before the most recent one.) So if his lack of long-term relationship success means something is the matter with him, then that's true for vast numbers of people.

Yes, Batman could learn to rely on other people more (to rely on *trustworthy* people, of course). He could become better at asking for help. The people in his inner circle would appreciate that. And if he relied more on the adults already in his life, perhaps he wouldn't end up taking on new young sidekicks and endangering their lives. Wayne, and his inner circle, might be able to think of other ways to mentor these at-risk youths, or the youths, like Stephanie Brown, who want to help. Surely a man this smart could think of safer alternatives for these teens.

He *is* odd and quirky. He does have issues. But almost all of us have issues. Like Wayne, having issues doesn't necessarily mean that we have a mental disorder. It means that we've got vulnerabilities, weaknesses, areas of our lives that could benefit from improvement. Such negative aspects are part of the nature of the human experience, and often are part of the range of "normal." It doesn't necessarily indicate "pathology."*

One could argue that the "symptoms" Wayne appears to have, along with some of his personality traits, enable Wayne to function as Batman as well as he does. Like Wayne, we all try to cope with the circumstances that life hands us; some "symptoms" or personality characteristics—ways of being in the world—can appear dysfunctional in one context, but be very adaptive and appropriate in another context. This too is part of the lesson that Batman teaches us.

---

* In fact, various forms of psychotherapy can be helpful even for issues and problems that don't reach the level of a "disorder."

ABOUT THE AUTHOR

Robin S. Rosenberg, Ph.D., is a clinical psychologist, board certified by the American Board of Professional Psychology, and a fellow of the American Academy of Clinical Psychology. Dr. Rosenberg enjoys using stories of superheroes and other popular culture figures to illustrate psychological principles and research. She is series editor of the *Superheroes* series with Oxford University Press and edited the anthologies *The Psychology of Superheroes* and *The Psychology of the Girl With the Dragon Tattoo*. She is also a blogger for *Huffington Post* and *Psychology Today*. She has been featured in a variety of media including the *Discovery*

Channel, the *History Channel,* the *Financial Times, Pacific Standard* magazine, *National Public Radio, The Boston Phoenix, The Philadelphia Inquirer, Newsarama,* and the documentary *Superheroes.* Dr. Rosenberg is also co-author of the psychology textbooks *Introducing Psychology* and *Abnormal Psychology.*

Dr. Rosenberg received her B.A. in psychology from New York University and her M.A. and Ph.D. in clinical psychology from the University of Maryland, College Park. She is President-Elect of the Santa Clara County Psychological Association.

ENDNOTES

Note: Some endnotes have more than one reference.

[1] Gotlib, I. H., & Robinson, L. A. (1982). Responses to depressed individuals: Discrepancies between self-report and observer rated behavior. *Journal of Abnormal Psychology, 91,* 231–240.

Segrin, C., & Abramson, L. Y. (1994). Negative reactions to depressive behaviors: communication theory analysis. *Journal Abnormal Psychology, 103,* 655–668.

[2] Kendler, K. S., Kuhn, J. W., Vittum, J., Prescott, C. A., & Riley, B. (2005). The interaction of stressful life events and a serotonin transporter polymorphism in the prediction of episodes of major depression: A replication. *Archives of General Psychiatry, 62,* 529–535.

Pilowsky, D.J., Wickramaratne, P., Talati, A., Tang, M. Hughes, C.W., Garber, J., et al. (2008). Children of depressed mothers a year after the initiation of maternal treatment: Findings from STAR*D-Child. *American Journal of Psychiatry, 165,* 1136–1147.

[3] Beck, A. (1967). *Depression.* New York: Harper & Row.

[4] Abramson, L. Y., Seligman, M. E., & Teasdale, J. D. (1978). Learned helplessness in humans: Critique and reformulation. *Journal of Abnormal Psychology, 87,* 49–74.

   Peterson, C., & Seligman, M. E. (1984). Causal explanations as a risk factor for depression: Theory and evidence. *Psychological Review, 91,* 347–374.

[5] Metalsky, G. I., Joiner, T. E., Hardin, T. S., & Abramson, L. Y. (1993). Depressive reactions to failure in a naturalistic setting: A test of the hopelessness and self-esteem theories of depression. *Journal of Abnormal Psychology, 102,* 101–109.

[6] Coyne, J. C. (1976). Toward an interactional description of depression. *Psychiatry: Journal for the Study of Interpersonal Processes, 39,* 28–40.

   Hsee, C. K., Hatfield, E., Carlson, J. G., & Chemtob, C. (1990). The effect of power on susceptibility to emotional contagion. *Cognition & Emotion, 4,* 327–340. http://transcripts.cnn.com/TRANSCRIPTS/0205/21/lt.24.html, accessed April 3, 2007.

[7] Joiner, T. E. (1994). Contagious depression: Existence, specificity to depressed symptoms, and the role of reassurance seeking. *Journal of Personality and Social Psychology, 67,* 287-296.

[8] Lewinsohn, P. M., Allen, N. B., Seeley, J. R., & Gotlib, I. H. (1999). First onset versus recurrence of depression:

Differential processes of psychosocial risk. *Journal of Abnormal Psychology, 108,* 483–489.

Tennant, C. (2002). Life events, stress and depression: A review of the findings. *Australian & New Zealand Journal of Psychiatry, 36,* 173–182.

[9] Weissman, M. M., Bland, R. C., Canino, G. J., Greenwald, S., Hwu, H. G., Lee, C. K., et al. (1994). The cross-national epidemiology of obsessive compulsive disorder: The Cross National Collaborative Group. *Journal of Clinical Psychiatry, 55,* 5–10.

[10] American Psychiatric Association (2000). *Diagnostic and Statistical Manual, Fourth Edition, Text Revision.* Washington, D.C.: American Psychiatric Press, p. 468.

[11] Breslau, N., Kessler, R. C., Chilcoat, H. D. Schultz, L. R., Davis, G. C., & Andreski, P. (1998). Trauma and posttraumatic stress disorder in the community: The 1996 Detroit Area Survey of Trauma. *Archives of General Psychiatry, 55,* 626–632.

Shalev, A. Y., Sahar, T., Freedman, S., Peri, T., Glick, N., Brandes, D., Orr, S. P., & Pitman, R. K. (1998). A prospective study of heart rate response following trauma and the subsequent development of posttraumatic stress disorder. *Archives of General Psychiatry, 55,* 553–559.

[12] Dikel, T. N., Engdahl, B., & Eberly, R. (2005). PTSD in former prisoners of war: Prewar, wartime, and postwar factors. *Journal of Traumatic Stress, 18,* 69–77.

[13] Brandes, D., Ben-Schachar, G., Gilboa, A., Bonne, O., Freedman, S., & Shalev, A. Y. (2002). PTSD symptoms and cognitive

performance in recent trauma survivors. *Psychiatry Research, 110*(3), 231-238.

[14] Ai, A. L., Cascio, T., Santangelo, L. K., & Evans-Campbell, T. (2005). Hope, meaning, and growth following the September 11, 2001, terrorist attacks. *Journal of Interpersonal Violence, 20,* 523–548.

Frankl, Viktor E. (1969). *The Will to Meaning: Foundations and Applications of Logotherapy.* New York: Meridian.

[15] Park, C. L. & Ai, A. L. (2006). Meaning making and growth: New directions for research on survivors of trauma. *Journal of Loss & Trauma, 11,* 389-407.

[16] Park, C. L. (2004). The notion of stress-related growth: Problems and prospects. *Psychological Inquiry, 15,* 69-76.

Reker, G. T., & Wong, P. T. P. (1988). Aging as an individual process: Toward a theory of personal meaning. In J. E. Birren & V. L. Bengston (Eds.), *Emergent Theories of Aging* (pp. 214–246). New York: Springer.

[17] Emmons, R. A. (2003). Personal goals, life meaning, and virtue: Wellsprings of a positive life. In Keyes, Corey L. M. (Ed); Haidt, Jonathan (Ed), *Flourishing: Positive Psychology and the Life Well-Lived.* (pp. 105-128). Washington, DC: American Psychological Association.

[18] Baumeister, Roy F. (1991). *Meanings of Life.* New York: The Guilford Press

[19] Janoff-Bulman, R. & Frantz, C. M. (1997). The impact of trauma on meaning: From meaningless world to meaningful life. In M. Power & C. R. Brewin. (Eds.), *The Transformation of Meaning in Psychological Therapies: Integrating Theory*

and Practice. Sussex: Wiley & Sons.

[20] Tedeschi, R. G., & Calhoun, L. (2004). Posttraumatic growth: Conceptual foundations and empirical evidence. *Psychological Inquiry, 15,* 1-15.

Updegraff, J. A., & Taylor, S. E. (2000). From vulnerability to growth: Positive and negative effects of stressful life events. In J. H. Harvey & E. Miller (Eds.). *Loss and trauma: General and close relationship perspectives*. (pp. 3-28). Philadelphia: Brunner-Routledge.

[21] Hare, R. D. (1993). *Without Conscience: The Disturbing World of the Psychopaths Among Us*. New York: Simon & Schuster.